Y0-AGS-121

EXTRAORDINARY LIVING

EIGHT STEPS to Improving Your Life

MARK CROW

EXTRAORDINARY LIVING

EIGHT STEPS to Improving Your Life

MARK CROW

HONOR NET
THE HONOR NETWORK

Extraordinary Living: Eight Steps to Improving Your Life

ISBN 10: 1-9331885-1-0
ISBN 13: 978-1-9331885-1-5

Copyright © 2007 by Mark Crow

Printed in the United States of America.

Published by HonorNet
PO Box 910
Sapulpa, OK 74067
Web site: honornet.net

DEDICATION

This book is dedicated to all of you who have prayed for me and believed in me. Life would not be extraordinary without you.

CONTENTS

FOREWORD

Y EARS AGO, THERE WAS AN OLD DISCOUNT SHOPPING center that I passed frequently. One day a sign was put up ... Victory Christian Center.

Not long after, an extraordinary church began to form, and then a new large sanctuary was built. I attended the church often and became friends with an extraordinary pastor, Mark Crow.

Then one day I turned on the television and heard an extraordinary sermon by an extremely extraordinary preacher. I went to lunch with this extraordinary pastor, and he began to tell me of his dreams for the future. I have watched as those dreams have become reality through satellite churches, new ministries, and countless people who are being reached by the Gospel of Jesus Christ.

When he sent me his new book, I knew that it would be extraordinary ... simply because of the way the man is. As I read the book, I thought only Mark Crow would use an illustration by John Wooden on how to put your socks on and weave it into a sermon that would bring extraordinary living ... from a very simple daily task.

This book will bless you and change you, and I know you will want to pass it on to a friend.

Someone once said, "Evangelism is one hungry man telling another hungry man where to find bread." This book is "extraordinary bread."

—Larry Jones
Feed the Children

ACKNOWLEDGMENTS

I N THE EARLY 1980S, I WALKED ON THE GROUNDS OF Oral Roberts University. Something happened there that I had never experienced before: I began to imagine, to dream. In those brief moments on that incredible campus, I realized that the world was far bigger than the world in which I was currently living and that God had more for me than I had previously imagined. It was as though the very architecture was designed to make a person see beyond the moment—beyond the "now" and into the future. And it was in that place that I began to see *my* future.

I would like to thank Oral Roberts and his late wife Evelyn and Richard and Lindsey Roberts for giving their lives to help me find my way to God's future for me. Oral Roberts University helped me to see what "could be" in my life. Today, I am living my dream because I came to realize that God had an extraordinary future for me, far bigger than my original expectations. It was at that great institution that I began to "Expect a Miracle." Thanks for pointing me to miracles.

INTRODUCTION

GOD HAS AN EXTRAORDINARY LIFE PLANNED FOR you! John 10:10 tells us that Jesus came to bring us abundant life—here and now, on this earth. Are you living in God's abundant life? Or are you living life burdened by past sin, broken relationships, financial challenges, and other problems?

It's time to change your life! Maybe you chose to make Jesus your personal Lord and Savior. Or maybe you believe that God is calling you to a new level in your spiritual walk. Whatever the case, this book is for you! It's easy to make a choice for change—but it's more challenging to walk that choice out in your daily life. That's what *Extraordinary Living* is all about—taking the steps you need to take in order to bring about amazing changes in your life!

I challenge you to take this time to follow the steps outlined in this book—steps that will lead you to an extraordinary life. Read each chapter and spend time meditating on the Scriptures at the end of each chapter. Allow the passages from God's Word to begin to transform your life in ways you never dreamed possible. Make a commitment to never settle for less, in any area of your life. Take the challenge—your extraordinary life awaits!

With the goodness of God to desire our highest welfare, the wisdom of God to plan it, and the power of God to achieve it, what do we lack?

A. W. Tozer

STEP 1
REVELATION:

EXTRAORDINARY GOD

S EVERAL YEARS AGO, EDWARD FARRELL OF DETROIT took his two-week vacation to Ireland to celebrate his son's favorite uncle's eightieth birthday. On the morning of the great day, Ed and his uncle got up before dawn, dressed in silence, and went for a walk along the shores of Lake Killarney. Just as the sun rose, his uncle turned and stared straight at the rising orb. Ed stood beside him for twenty minutes with not a single word exchanged. Then the elderly uncle began to skip along the shoreline, a radiant smile on his face.

After catching up with him, Ed commented, "Uncle Seamus, you look very happy. Do you want to tell me why?"

"Yes, lad," the old man said, tears washing down his face. "You see, the Father is fond of me. Ah, me Father is so very fond of me."

Uncle Seamus had an understanding of God that, sadly, many Christians lack. He realized how great the Father's love was for *him*, personally. Do you have that kind of relationship with God? Do you realize just how much He loves and cares for *you*?

David Redding wrote:

> There is no other blessing I can give you, no gift so precious, no treasure so refreshing, nothing that can give you provision for the journey we are all making, than to tell you that Someone is searching diligently for you. He is not a stationary God. *He is crazy about you.* The expense to which He has gone isn't reasonable, is it? The Cross was not a very dignified ransom. To say the least, it was a splurge of love and glory lavishly spent on you and me: "While we were yet sinners, Christ died for the ungodly." "A shepherd having a hundred sheep, if he loses one, leaves the ninety-nine to go after the one and searches diligently until he finds it."
>
> God is like that shepherd. That is enough to make me laugh and cry.[1]

Living the extraordinary life begins by having an extraordinary revelation of who God is. God is a good

God. The Bible says, *God is love* (1 John 4:16). Many people do not have this revelation of God's character. They have never been introduced to a loving God, and so it is hard for them to love God in return.

But when you begin to understand who God really is and that His plans for your life are good, you will begin to live the extraordinary life that He wants you to live!

I have five children, and there isn't anything that they could ever do that would make me stop loving them. God is like that with us—we are His children, and nothing we could do would ever make Him stop loving us. God is very aware of where you are in your life and the things that you need. He wants you to turn to Him and look to Him as your Provider and Shepherd and Lord. He loves you, and He wants to have a relationship with you.

I USED TO PICTURE GOD AS AN ANGRY, VENGEFUL DEITY WHO WAS SAVING UP HIS WRATH TO POUR OUT ON ME AT ANY TIME.

Many people are afraid of God, but the Bible never says to "be afraid" of Him. Instead, it tells us to *fear the LORD your God...* (Deuteronomy 6:13 NKJV). In the original language, that phrase means "to hold Him in awe and respect." We must respect God, but it has never been God's heart for His children to be afraid of Him.

I used to be that way. I used to picture God as an angry, vengeful deity who was saving up His wrath to pour out on me at any time. Because that was my picture of God, I was afraid of Him—wouldn't you be? I didn't want to go to church, I didn't want to pray, I didn't want to even think about God. All I wanted to do was to live my life and somehow stay out of His way! But then, when I was in my twenties, something changed in my life. I received an amazing revelation—the revelation that God is a *God of love*! I began to see Him as Someone who would love me even when I messed up, when I fell down, when I did something dumb. He knew me—really *knew me*—and He loved me anyway. Not only that, but He was standing ready to meet my every need and to bless me with an extraordinary life, a life He had planned for me even before I was born.

Who Is God?

God wants all people everywhere to have a picture of Him as He really is. He longs for all of His children all over the world to know how much He loves them. Musician Michael Card once said in an interview, "Again and again in China, I talked to people who had never heard of Christianity, never heard of Jesus, never heard a single word from the Bible. Yet through nature and their God-given conscience, many believed in God. Not only did they believe God existed, they had even derived some understanding about His loving character because He provided food, water, and a beautiful world. One old woman told me, 'I've known Him for years. I just didn't know His name.'"[2] When these people received a revelation of who

God is—when they learned "His name"—they were able to begin a relationship with their Creator, the greatest relationship they would ever experience. They were able to embark on the journey to an *extraordinary life* because of that revelation.

Knowing God—knowing who He is and what His character is like—can change your life! In his classic book, *Knowing God*, J. I. Packer shares the impact that understanding God's amazing love had upon his Christian walk:

> What matters supremely, therefore, is not, in the last analysis, the fact that I know God, but the larger fact which underlies it—that He knows me. I am graven on the palms of His hands. I am never out of His mind. All my knowledge of Him depends on His sustained initiative in knowing me. I know Him because He first knew me, and continues to know me. He knows me as a friend, one who loves me; and there is no moment when His eye is off me, or His attention distracted from me, and no moment, therefore, when His care falters. This is momentous knowledge. There is unspeakable comfort…in knowing that God is constantly taking knowledge of me in love and watching over me for my good. There is tremendous relief in knowing that His love is utterly realistic, based at every point on prior knowledge of the worst about me, so that no discovery now can

disillusion Him about me, in the way I am so often disillusioned about myself, and quench His determination to bless me.[3]

Did you know that you can quench the blessings of God on your life if you do not understand His character and His desire to so richly bless you—far beyond what you deserve? That's why a true *revelation* of who God is is so important!

Without a Vision, the People Perish

Proverbs 29:18 says, *Where there is no revelation, the people cast off restraint* (NKJV). Another version states, *Where there is no vision, the people perish* (KJV). If we don't have a revelation of who God is, our lives will be adversely affected—we will not be able to live the extraordinary, abundant life that God has planned for us.

GOD IS A GOD WHO IS FULL OF LOVE AND LIFE, AND HE WANTS TO BESTOW BLESSINGS UPON HIS CHILDREN.

The Message words Proverbs 29:18 like this: *If people can't see what God is doing, they stumble all over themselves.* Religion clouds our picture of God. Legalism clouds our revelation of the Lord. We need a true picture of God and what He wants for our lives. Jesus gives it to us in John 10:10: *"I am come that they might have life, and that they might have it more abundantly"* (KJV). The *New*

International Version reads, *"I have come that they may have life, and have it to the full."* That's the picture of God we need to cling to: God is a God who is full of love and life, and He wants to bestow blessings upon His children.

Some people feel that their problems are too big for God to solve—or too small to capture His attention. Such was the case of a woman named Margaret, who did not realize that God wanted to honor her with blessings, both large and small.

Margaret did not want to go to the prayer service that evening; she wanted to stay home instead and make a dish of candied fruit from a new recipe. But the recipe called for three oranges, and she had none.

Reluctantly, Margaret decided to go to church, thinking that if she got the oranges that night, she could make the dish first thing in the morning. As she drove through the city to church, she stopped at every corner store along the way, looking for oranges. Unfortunately, all of the stores that she passed were out. Margaret arrived at church feeling disappointed but determined to keep her mind on the service until the end.

As she was leaving the church after the service was over, a teenage boy asked her for a ride home, and Margaret reluctantly agreed to take him. When they pulled into the public housing project where he lived, her headlights landed on a loaded pickup truck. As they drew in closer, Margaret shrieked, "Oranges!" There, spotlighted by a street lamp, stood a truckload of oranges—boxes and boxes of large, beautiful oranges.

"Where is the driver?" Margaret asked aloud.

"Here he comes now!" replied the teenager. Reaching hurriedly into her purse and finding one dollar, she gave it to the teenager and told him to ask the man if she could buy three oranges. He jumped out as Margaret craned her head out the window trying to see around the truck. She was still holding her breath when the boy came around the truck with as many oranges in his arms as he could carry.

"He didn't have any bags!" called the boy.

Awed and overjoyed, Margaret took the fruit, returning several to the grateful teen. That night, she made her candied fruit, knowing that because she had put God first, He had showered His blessings upon her.

Unlike Margaret, some people feel that they don't deserve to live the abundant life that God wants them to live. They feel that their sin is too great, and they don't feel worthy of any blessings in their lives. The good news is that none of us are worthy of living this abundant life! How is that good news? It's good news because through Jesus, we *have been made* worthy. He paid the price for our sins and made it possible for us to have a relationship with an extraordinary God who wants us to live extraordinary lives!

Salvation is by faith. We can't be saved without a revelation of our sin and our need for God. But we also can't be saved without a revelation of the goodness of God and what He did to purchase our salvation. This revelation will cause our walk with Him to be filled with blessings because we begin to grasp the lengths to which God would go to cause us to live an abundant life.

In Galatians 3:23-25, the Bible says, *Before this faith came, we were all held prisoners by the law. We had no freedom until God showed us the way of faith that was coming. In other words, the law was our guardian leading us to Christ so that we could be made right with God through faith. Now the way of faith has come, and we no longer live under a guardian* (NCV). In other words, you and I can never be justified by our works; we are justified only by our faith in Jesus Christ. Salvation is by faith, and we need to have a revelation of our need for a Savior.

The devil doesn't want us to receive this revelation from God. He doesn't want us to know that we can be forgiven. He doesn't want us to know that God wants to do great things in our lives. He wants us to believe that, even if we can be saved, we are not going to live beyond that salvation. He wants us to believe that for the length of time that we are on this earth, we will have to live under the dominion and influence of darkness. But we don't have to live in darkness! Ephesians 5:8 says, *For you were once darkness, but now you are light in the Lord. Live as children of light....* The influence of darkness will begin to diminish as the influence of the light and the glorious gospel of Jesus Christ is elevated in our lives!

Such was the case in the life of a suicidal atheist, whom God reached out to in his time of desperate need. One of the first persons to enter the New Life Treatment Center in Belleville, Washington, was a confirmed atheist. One night he flew into a suicidal rage, and out of desperation, he sought a phone book to find the number of a psychiatrist. At 3:00 a.m., few psychiatrists were available, but the one at the New Life Treatment Center answered her phone. She instructed the desperate man to come to the center that night. He did so, but when he woke up the next morning, he commented that if there were a God, then He had played a terrible trick on him by landing him in a Christian treatment center. It was tough for him to stay, but he struggled and managed to make it to the fourth day.

JESUS IS TRUTH, AND HE DEMONSTRATES TO US THE TRUTH OF WHO GOD IS AND WHO HE CAN BE IN OUR LIVES.

On the evening of the fourth day, the man accompanied the other alcoholic patients to an Alcoholics Anonymous meeting. At the end of the meeting, a young boy stood up and asked for help. He told them he was suicidal—he said that he was visualizing, in full color, putting a gun to his head and pulling the trigger. The atheist could relate to the boy since he had been in the same frame of mind just four days earlier.

When the boy sat down, silence filled the room. Suddenly, the back door of the room opened and a strange-looking man walked in wearing what looked like a turban and a hospital-issued robe. He said that his wife and kids were in the car, but that he felt God wanted him to come into the room and say something. He had not heard the boy who had just relayed his thoughts of suicide, but he said, "If anyone here is thinking of killing himself, I want to encourage you to reconsider. God loves you and wants you to live. This turban on my head is a bandage from where I put a gun to my own head and pulled the trigger. Fortunately, I survived so that I could come here and tell you not to do it. God loves you."

That day the atheist patient found God.

God will do what it takes to bring truth into our lives. Jesus said, *"You will know the truth, and the truth will make you free"* (John 8:32 NCV). He also said, *"I am the way, and the truth, and the life. The only way to the Father is through me"* (John 14:6 NCV). Jesus is Truth, and He demonstrates to us the truth of who God is and who He can be in our lives. Without that truth, without the Living Truth inside of us, we will perish.

When England closed its Libyan Embassy in the 1980s, Muammar Qaddafi became so angry that he ordered England to be removed from all maps in Libya! To this day, if you buy a map in that country, the area usually set aside to depict Great Britain will be represented by a new arm of the North Sea bordered by Scotland and Wales. I can only imagine what a sailor from Libya would think if he crossed the North Sea, expecting the waters to continue, and instead suddenly encountered the European continent! That is what it means to have an *incorrect revelation* of truth. Finding out the truth—receiving a revelation of who God really is—is extremely important to every area of our lives.

Finding the Truth

We need to find out the truth—and then we need to live it out! Many Christians don't even know what's in the Bible. We need to get into the Word for ourselves and not just trust what someone else tells us is in the Bible. I am sure you have heard the saying, "God helps those who help themselves." This sounds good, but this saying is not actually found in the Bible. Although it can be true that faith moves God, this quote leans toward works and not grace. The devil quoted the Bible to Jesus when He was being tempted—except he did not quote it in its entirety. He took things out of context to try to trip Jesus up, but he failed because Jesus knew the Word. It's the same way for the rest of us. The devil will misquote the Word to us, and if we are ignorant of the Word, we will believe what he says. We need a revelation of an extraordinary God, and we have to know His extraordinary Word before we can lead an extraordinary life.

One day Jesus turned to His disciples and asked, "Who do people say that I am?"

> When Jesus came to the region of Caesarea Philippi, he asked his disciples, "Who do people say the Son of Man is?"

They replied, "Some say John the Baptist; others say Elijah; and still others, Jeremiah or one of the prophets."

"But what about you?" he asked. "Who do you say I am?"

Simon Peter answered, "You are the Christ, the Son of the living God."

Jesus replied, "Blessed are you, Simon son of Jonah, for this was not revealed to you by man, but by my Father in heaven. And I tell you that you are Peter, and on this rock I will build my church, and the gates of Hades will not overcome it. I will give you the keys of the kingdom of heaven; whatever you bind on earth will be bound in heaven, and whatever you loose on earth will be loosed in heaven." Then He warned his disciples not to tell anyone that he was the Christ.

MATTHEW 16:13-20

Jesus asks the same question of you today: "Who do *you* say that I am?" Who is Jesus to you? Is He your Provider? Is He your Healer? Is He your Savior? Who is He to you?

He's not asking this question of your mother or father, or your pastor or friends. Their faith is not going to give you what you need. He's asking the question of you. You can step up and say, "Jesus, You are everything today that You have always been. You're my Savior. You're my Deliverer. You're my Provider. You're the Protector of my soul. You're everything You've ever been. That's who I say You are. You're everything to me."

Jacqueline was a woman who truly caught the *revelation* of God's love and care for her. It took some time, however, and, ultimately, a word from God Himself.

Jacqueline was an elderly woman who lived to take care of her daughter, who was wheelchair-bound. When her daughter died, Jacqueline not only lost her purpose for living, but she also lost her living companion. Her cottage in the country seemed as empty as an eggshell. Occasionally a friend would call or a note would arrive, but most of her time was spent in oppressive, ongoing solitude. Her health didn't allow her to get out among other people very much, and her best friends were now all in heaven.

> "JESUS LOVES ME, THIS I KNOW, FOR THE BIBLE TELLS ME SO."

One day, Jacqueline sat down with her Bible and it fell open to Philippians 4:5, where four words struck her forcibly: *The Lord is near. If so*, thought Jacqueline, *I should be more aware of it.*

"Lord," she said, "I'm going to pretend You're here all the time. No, forgive me for using that word; there is no *pretending* to be done. I'm going to use my God-given imagination to visualize how very present You really are. Help me to ever *remind myself* of the reality of Your nearness."

That evening as she prepared for bed, she said, "I'm going on to bed now, Lord. Will You please watch over me as I sleep?" The next morning upon awakening, she said, "Good morning, Lord! This is the day that You have made!" Sitting down with her hot tea that morning, she read through the book of Philippians again, underlining verse 5 of chapter 4, then she prayed aloud for a very long time. At noon, she said, "Now, Lord, let's watch the news on television so that You can show me things in this world I can pray for." Jacqueline and the Lord watched the news together as she prayed for flood victims in the Delta, for a newly installed president in an African country, and for a man sentenced to life imprisonment.

At supper, she bowed her head and thanked the Lord for her food, but somehow she didn't feel that her prayers were traveling up to heaven. She felt instead that she was talking to Someone who was actually sitting across the table from her.

Gradually, her entire attitude was transformed. The loneliness lessened, her joy increased, her fear diminished, and she never again felt that she was alone in her house. Jacqueline had received a fresh, new revelation of who God was to her, and it changed her entire life.

Karl Barth, the famed theologian who wrote many doctrinal treatises and debated many complex theological issues in his lifetime, was once asked, "What is the greatest thought you ever had?" His answer was simple, yet profound, providing the greatest revelation the world has ever known: "Jesus loves me, this I know, for the Bible tells me so."

When you catch the revelation of who Jesus is to you and how much He loves you, your life will begin to change—and not only yours but also the lives of the people around you. Some of you may see Jesus as your ticket out of hell, and He certainly is that. But more than that, Jesus is your ticket to an extraordinary life.

Extraordinary Word

Read and/or memorize the following Scripture passages, allowing them to transform your life.

▸ *Where there is no vision, the people perish* (Proverbs 29:18 KJV).

▸ Jesus said… *"I have come that they may have life, and that they may have it more abundantly"* (John 10:10 NKJV).

▸ *Beloved, let us love one another, for love is of God; and everyone who loves is born of God and knows God. He who does not love does not know God, for God is love* (1 John 4:7–8 NKJV).

▸ *In the beginning was the Word, and the Word was with God, and the Word was God. He was with God in the beginning. Through him all things were made; without him nothing was made that has been made. In him was life, and that life was the light of men* (John 1:1-4).

▸ *Before this faith came, we were all held prisoners by the law. We had no freedom until God showed us the way of faith that was coming. In other words, the law was our guardian leading us to Christ so that we could be made right with God through faith. Now the way of faith has come, and we no longer live under a guardian* (Galatians 3:23-25 NCV).

▸ *Jesus [said], "I am the way, and the truth, and the life. The only way to the Father is through me"* (John 14:6 NCV).

▸ *Jesus said…"You will know the truth, and the truth will make you free"* (John 8:31-32 NCV).

Extraordinary Focus

▸ Have you caught, truly caught, the revelation of God's amazing love for *you*? If not, what can you do to open yourself up to His love today?

▸ Have you ever been afraid of God? If so, what was the reason? What is the difference between the Bible's idea of the "fear of God" and man's idea? How can you begin to draw closer to God in respect rather than fear?

▶   Who is Jesus in *your* life? What changes has knowing Him brought about for you?

Extraordinary Action

Ask yourself the question, "Who do *I* say that Jesus is?" In a notebook or a personal journal, write a prayer to the Lord, expressing who He is to you and what He means to your life.

Repentance: That mighty change in mind, heart, and life wrought by the Spirit of God.

RICHARD TRENCH
ARCHBISHOP OF DUBLIN

STEP 2
REPENTANCE:

EXERCISING
EXTRAORDINARY FAITH

JIMMY HAD TROUBLE PRONOUNCING THE LETTER "R" so his teacher gave him a sentence to practice at home: "Robert gave Richard a rap in the rib for roasting the rabbit so rare."

Some days later, the teacher asked him to say the sentence for her. Jimmy rattled it off like this: "Bob gave Dick a poke in the side for not cooking the bunny enough." He had completely evaded the letter "R."

There are a lot of people today—including many Christians—who go to great lengths to avoid the "R" word of *repentance*, but repentance is absolutely necessary to bring us into the extraordinary life that God has for us. Extraordinary living was brought to us by Jesus Christ. Because of Jesus, we can live the abundant life that God has for us. The first step toward that abundant life is to receive a *revelation* of who God is and the amazing things He wants to do in our lives, and the second step is *repentance.*

> *"Therefore, O house of Israel, I will judge you, each one according to his ways, declares the Sovereign LORD. Repent! Turn away from all your offenses; then sin will not be your downfall. Rid yourselves of all the offenses you have committed, and get a new heart and a new spirit. Why will you die, O house of Israel? For I take no pleasure in the death of anyone, declares the Sovereign LORD. Repent and live!"*
>
> EZEKIEL 18:30–32

THE KINGDOM OF GOD—GOD'S EXTRAORDINARY LIFE FOR YOU AND FOR ME—IS NEAR!

Even in the Old Testament, it is clear that God does not take pleasure in the death of anyone; instead, He pleads with His people: "Repent and live!" Frederica Mathewes-Green has this to say about repentance: "The first time Jesus appears, in the first Gospel, the first instruction He gives is 'Repent.' From then on, it's His most consistent message. In all times and in every situation, His advice is to repent. Not just to the scribes and the Pharisees, not just to the powerful—He tells even the poor and oppressed that repentance is the key to eternal life."[1]

Repentance Defined

What is repentance? It is simply a turning around, a changing of the way you would like to think and behave and, instead, thinking and behaving according to the ways of God. Vince Havner said, "Repentance is a change of mind about sin and self and the Savior."[2] A. W. Tozer adds, "A thousand years of remorse over a wrong act would not please God as much as a change of conduct and a reformed life."[3]

In Matthew 3 and 4, both Jesus and John the Baptist declared: *"Repent, for the kingdom of heaven is near."* Neither of them was sharing this truth to put fear in the people, but to stir up hope within them. The kingdom of God—God's extraordinary life for you and for me— is near! But repentance is required to participate in this kingdom.

I grew up in a church where we would work ourselves into an emotional frenzy, and then people would "respond" to God. But when they left the church service and returned to their everyday lives, they were not changed. Why? Because they had not fully thought through what they were doing. God gave us a brain—and He wants us to use our brain to make choices (He also gave us free will!) that will benefit our lives.

Most of us think of repentance as one-dimensional, something emotional that once happened to us in a church service. But true repentance, while it can be emotional, is more of a choice that we make to turn away from the things that are tearing us down, and to turn toward the things that would lift us up. And true repentance results in true change.

When Michigan played Wisconsin in basketball early in the season in 1989, Michigan's Rumeal Robinson stepped to the foul line for two shots late in the fourth quarter. His team trailed by one point, so Rumeal could conceivably regain the lead for Michigan. Unfortunately, he missed both shots, allowing Wisconsin to upset the favored team, Michigan.

Rumeal felt terrible about costing his team the game, but his sorrow didn't stop at the emotional level. After each practice for the rest of the season, Rumeal shot one hundred extra foul shots. Thus, Rumeal was ready when he stepped to the foul line to shoot two shots with three seconds left in overtime in the national-championship game.

Swish went the first shot, and swish went the second. Those shots won Michigan the national championship. Rumeal's "repentance" had been genuine, and his sorrow motivated him to work so that he would never make that mistake again. As Paul wrote, *Godly sorrow brings repentance that leads to salvation* (2 Corinthians 7:10).

Acts 3:19 tells us, *"Now change your mind and attitude to God and turn to him so he can cleanse away your sins and send you wonderful times of refreshment from the presence of the Lord"* (TLB). We are to change both our minds and our attitudes. The word *repentance* in the Greek means "to think differently." There is a change that takes place!

In *Mission in Christ's Way*, Lesslie Newbigin, long-time missionary to India, wrote about the true meaning of repentance:

> I remember once visiting a village in the Madras diocese. There was no road into the village; you reached it by crossing a river, and you could not do this either on the south side of the village or on the north. The congregation had decided that I would come by the southern route, and they had prepared a welcome such as only an Indian village can prepare. There was music and fireworks and garlands and fruit—everything you can imagine. Unfortunately, I entered the village at the north end and found only a few goats and chickens. Crisis! I had to disappear while word was sent to the assembled congregation, and the entire village did a sort of U-turn so as to face the other way. Then I duly reappeared.
>
> This is what *metanola* [the word *repent*] means. The TEV translation gives a misleading impression by translating it: "Turn away from

your sins." That might make it look like a traditional call for moral reformation. That is not the point. There is nothing about sins in the text (Mark 1:14–18). The point is: "The reign of God has drawn near, but you can't see it because you are looking the wrong way. You are expecting the wrong thing. What you think is "God" isn't God at all. You have to be, as Paul says, transformed by the renewing of your mind. You have to go through a mental revolution; otherwise the reign of God will be totally hidden from you.[4]

True repentance begins to understand that you are not just trying to get out of the mess that you're in, but you are stepping into what God offers you—the abundant, extraordinary life that comes through Jesus Christ. What a waste it would be to go before God at the end of your life and say, "Here I am, Lord. I gave You my heart, and You saved me from my sin. I'm so glad to finally be here, because life has just been miserable." No! That's not what God has planned for you! Jesus paid not just for your eternity in heaven, but for your abundant, extraordinary life here on this earth! In other words, you now have the opportunity to turn away from the things

REGARDLESS OF WHAT ADVERSITY YOU FACE, YOU CAN STILL KNOW THE EXTRAORDINARY LIFE, IF YOU MAKE THE *CHOICE* TO DO SO.

that are consuming you and dominating your life, and turn to the amazing things that God has planned for you. Regardless of what adversity you face, you can still know the extraordinary life, if you make the *choice* to do so.

Coming to Our Senses

Most of us are familiar with the story of the Prodigal Son, found in Luke 15:

> *"There was a man who had two sons. The younger one said to his father, 'Father, give me my share of the estate.' So he divided his property between them.*
>
> *"Not long after that, the younger son got together all he had, set off for a distant country and there squandered his wealth in wild living. After he had spent everything, there was a severe famine in that whole country, and he began to be in need. So he went and hired himself out to a citizen of that country, who sent him to his fields to feed pigs. He longed to fill his stomach with the pods that the pigs were eating, but no one gave him anything.*
>
> *"When he came to his senses, he said, 'How many of my father's hired men have food to spare, and here I am starving to death! I will set out and go back to my father and say to him: Father, I*

have sinned against heaven and against you. I am no longer worthy to be called your son; make me like one of your hired men. So he got up and went to his father.

"But while he was still a long way off, his father saw him and was filled with compassion for him; he ran to his son, threw his arms around him and kissed him.

"The son said to him, 'Father, I have sinned against heaven and against you. I am no longer worthy to be called your son.'

"But the father said to his servants, 'Quick! Bring the best robe and put it on him. Put a ring on his finger and sandals on his feet. Bring the fattened calf and kill it. Let's have a feast and celebrate. For this son of mine was dead and is alive again; he was lost and is found.' So they began to celebrate."

LUKE 15:11-24

The prodigal son had been born into a wealthy household. He had been given an inheritance. But rather than waiting until his father died to receive the money, he demanded the inheritance up front, and then went out and squandered the money on wild living. When he finally came to the end of himself, the Bible says: *"He came to his senses [and] said, 'How many of my father's hired men have food to spare, and here I am starving to death!'"* He had a *revelation*—and it resulted in a *change* in his thinking.

Now, I hope that you don't have to come to the end of your rope before you change the way that you think! I have heard it said, "Follow the light. Don't wait to hit the rocks!" The reason there are lighthouses is to prevent ships from crashing into the rocks and cliffs along the shore. The Light of Hope, the light of Jesus Christ has been given to us so that we can live an extraordinary life—not being dashed against the rocks of adversity, but putting ourselves in a place where we can follow the illumination of God's Spirit who will guide us into all the wonderful things that God has for us.

When the prodigal son "came to his senses," what did he do? He said to himself: *I'm going back to my father. I'll say to him, "Father, I have sinned against God. I've sinned before you. I don't deserve to be called your son. Take me on as a servant, as a hired hand."* That repentance, that turning, that change of thinking, brought him back into the place that he belonged.

Obviously, this parable refers to you and to me and to our relationship with our heavenly Father. When we repent and turn back to Him, what does He say? "Bring the fattened calf! Let's have a celebration!" In other words, He declares, "I want to pour out My blessings on this, My child, who has returned to Me. I want him to experience an abundant, extraordinary life!"

Change Your Heart

It's critical to change your thoughts, your mind, and your attitude, because your thoughts will ultimately determine your change of heart. And your heart holds the key to your blessings here on earth. Proverbs 23:7 says, *For as he thinks in his heart, so is he* (NKJV). How does a man think in his heart? By first allowing the words and thoughts in his mind to seep down into his heart. Proverbs 4:23 warns, *Above all else, guard your heart, for it is the wellspring of life.* In 2 Corinthians 10:5-6, Paul instructed, *We demolish arguments and every pretension that sets itself up against the knowledge of God, and we take captive every thought to make it obedient to Christ.* Why did Paul tell us to take every thought captive? Because if your negative thoughts are allowed to mature, they will ultimately become your master. They will get into the fabric of your heart, and every person ultimately lives out of what is in his heart.

IN OTHER WORDS, OUR HEART ATTITUDE WILL EITHER LEAD US INTO THE EXTRAORDINARY LIFE GOD HAS FOR US—OR AWAY FROM IT.

Words cannot adequately describe the incredible impact of our heart attitude on our lives. The longer I live, the more convinced I become that life is 10 percent what happens to us and 90 percent how we respond to it.

I believe the single most significant decision we can make on a day-to-day basis is our *choice* of attitude. It is more important than our past, our education, the amount of money in our bank account, our successes or failures, our fame or pain, what other people think of us or say about us, our circumstances, or our positions in life. Our heart attitudes will keep us going or cripple our progress. When our heart attitude is right, there is no barrier too high, no valley too deep, no dream too extreme, and no challenge too great for us. In other words, our heart attitude will either lead us into the extraordinary life God has for us—or away from it.

You and I must constantly commit our thoughts to the Lord on a daily, even an hourly, basis. Ask Him, "Lord, is this thought a good thought, or is it a bad thought? Does this thought glorify You? Does this thought benefit Your kingdom, or does it hurt it? Does this thought benefit my life, or will it bring destruction into my life?"

Romans 10:10 tells us, *For it is by believing in your heart that you are made right with God* (NLT). When the Bible refers to a man's heart, it refers to the whole man, his innermost being. It is the point of man where everything about him comes into play (thoughts, emotions, passions, fears, etc.). It is the center of his being and the place where God dwells.

In Matthew 15:18, Jesus said, *"But the things that come out of the mouth come from the heart."* In other words, they come in through our thoughts, through our brains, seep down into our hearts, and eventually come out of our mouths. To what kind of thoughts was Jesus referring? *"These make a man 'unclean.' For out of the heart come evil thoughts, murder, adultery, sexual immorality, theft, false testimony, slander. These are what make a man 'unclean'"* (verses 18-20).

Paul put it this way in Ephesians 1:18: *I pray also that the eyes of your heart may be enlightened in order that you may know the hope to which he has called you, the riches of his glorious inheritance in the saints.* Once you recognize that the blessings of God were brought to earth through Christ for you, you will want to change your way of thinking and being. You will want to turn toward the things of God, the things of blessing, life, and abundance.

The Key to Repentance

The story is told of a shoplifter who writes to a department store and says, "I've just become a Christian, and I can't sleep at night because I feel guilty. So, here's $100 that I owe you." Then he signs his name, but in a tiny postscript at the bottom, he adds, "If I still can't sleep tonight, I'll send you the rest."

Unfortunately, that is not a true attitude of repentance! God expects change, a complete turning from that which is bad (or sinful) to that which is good (or righteous).

In direct contrast was the revival that broke out in May 2001, when English evangelist J. John spoke in Liverpool, England, on one of the Ten Commandments: You shall not steal. The results of the preaching were dramatic. Here is what one of the newspaper reports had to say about what happened:

> Conscience-stricken people have handed in large quantities of stolen goods, including hotel towels, a bathrobe, and cash, after attending a church rally at which a preacher urged them to repent.
>
> The inventory of pilfered items included hospital crutches, library books, CDs, video-tapes—and about $560 [U.S.]. There were also several letters of confession.
>
> The items were left in large special containers at the Anglican cathedral in Liverpool, northern England, after May 15 when a congregation of 3,000 heard renowned preacher J. John speak at the cathedral on the Eighth Commandment: "Thou shalt not steal."
>
> John, 43, has been preaching on the Ten Commandments in a series of meetings in Liverpool.
>
> John said goods are commonly handed in after his meetings, with stolen items ranging from computers to shovels.
>
> "Stealing any item, however small, is wrong. The commandment doesn't say, 'Don't steal over one pound [sterling] at a time," John said.

"A man who is now a vicar took towels from the Wimbledon tennis championships years ago when he was working there. He kept them all these years and has now returned them."[5]

This same concept is illustrated by the letters that pour in to the U.S. government every day. In 1811, the government began collecting and storing letters like the following note dated February 6, 1974: "I am sending ten dollars for blankets I stole while in World War II. My mind could not rest. Sorry I'm late." It was signed: An ex-GI. And there was this postscript: "I want to be ready to meet with God."

> THE KEY TO REPENTANCE IS NOT ABOUT *BEING* RIGHT; IT'S SIMPLY ABOUT *GETTING* RIGHT.

The U.S. government not only collects and stores these letters, but the Treasury Department established a fund and labeled it the "Conscience Fund." Since its inception, the fund has grown to almost seven million dollars.

That is true repentance.

The key to repentance is not about *being* right; it's simply about *getting* right. It's about getting yourself in a position for God to do something extraordinary. Repentance doesn't mean perfection; it means setting yourself on course for the abundant life. When you are born again, when you repent, when you begin to look to God to give you His extraordinary life, you will suddenly find yourself with a new purpose and a passion for life that you never had before. And when you have purpose and passion, it doesn't matter what else is going on in your life, because you know that God has an abundant, extraordinary life for you, and you will settle for nothing less!

Kimberly, a self-proposed "witch" and opponent of the Gospel, entered a church one night, seeking answers. Her life had been falling apart, and she knew that the things she was doing weren't working.

As she sat down, she silently shot up a desperate prayer: *God, please give me someone in this crazy crowd I can relate to. If You don't give me someone, I'm walking out of here.* At that moment, the pastor told the congregation to stand up and shake a few hands. Kimberly introduced herself to Lisa, whose dyed-red hair and nose ring suggested that they might be at a similar place. Kimberly's black-and-white hair and spiked belt told her the same. Lisa, a fellow spiritual seeker, and Kimberly became fast friends.

Looking back, Kimberly wondered how the church members stood having her in their midst for so long. She was angry and exasperated as she sat listening to their "good news." How could there be only one way to God? At the end of each message, she marched down the aisle to the pastor and began firing off an onslaught of questions. After three or four weeks of verbal sparring, he humbly offered the associate pastor's ear. Kimberly made her rounds from one elder to another, finally ending up at a Friday night Bible study looking for answers.

As she sat on the floor in the leader's living room, she felt a peace amidst this group of people who seemed to care about each other. After the study, Lisa sat beside Kimberly as Scott, the leader, patiently listened to her New-Age arguments. But one by one, the Scriptures Kimberly had carefully prepared to punch holes in the Gospel came back at her with hurricane force. Scott's words—but especially the Bible's words—confounded her cosmic view. After they'd sat there for an hour debating, Kimberly was exhausted. Her hardened heart and argumentative nature had finally had enough.

As Lisa drove her home, Kimberly's mind ached as she replayed Scott's words. All the Old Testament and New Testament verses had one oddly familiar voice—one tone, one heart. She wondered, *How could a book written by so many different people over the course of hundreds of years fit together perfectly as if one amazing storyteller had written the whole thing?* The Holy Spirit began melting her vanity and arrogance with a power stronger than any hex, incantation, or spell she'd ever used. Suddenly, the blindfold she'd worn for almost thirty years was stripped away, and instantly she knew what she'd been searching for: *Jesus!* The same God she'd neglected, whose name she had used as profanity, whom she had flat-out rejected, was the One who'd sent His Son to suffer for her, to take the guilty verdict so that she could be found innocent. Kimberly's eyes filled with tears as she exchanged the darkness with which she'd grown so accustomed for the light of God's truth. It was such a personal moment between her and the Lord that even Lisa, sitting next to her in the car, had no idea what was going on.

But the story didn't end there. Kimberly soon realized that her life was filled with empty props, and it was time to clean house. Her first act of obedience was to throw out all of her books on witchcraft and the paranormal, as well as her tarot cards. But her most important possession—and the most difficult to discard—was her treasured crystal ball.

Kimberly called Lisa. She came right over, and the two friends immediately drove to the Pacific Ocean. Kimberly's heart pounded as if the demons themselves weren't far behind them. They stood at the end of the Malibu Pier, their beaming faces reflecting the radiance of the setting sun. Kimberly unwrapped the crystal's black velvet cover, and light streamed out like rainbows as the thick crystal met the sun's fleeting rays. As she dropped the ball into the deep blue water, she knew her future was secure. Now she had a Savior who would be with her always. Her repentance had "sealed the deal" between her and God.

It is time for repentance. It is time to examine yourself and make a change of judgment in your life. The movie *Les Miserables*, based on the novel by Victor Hugo, opens with a vagabond curled up on a stone bench on a desolate French street corner. His bedraggled appearance makes him seem dangerous and causes the townspeople, from whom he sought food and shelter, to snub him. Finally he slumps over in dejection—until a passerby points to a place where he can find refuge.

He goes to the door and knocks. The homeowner, the town's bishop, is startled by the late-night visitation but attentively listens to his story. His name is Jean Valjean, and he reveals that he is a recently released convict and marked by the authorities as dangerous. Even so, the bishop welcomes him into his home and serves him dinner.

Later, in the middle of the night, despite the bishop's kindness, Valjean double-crosses him. Valjean remembers the sparkling silver spoon he used to eat his soup at dinner and sneaks to the dining room to steal the bishop's valuable silverware. The clanking of metal arouses the bishop, who rises to inspect the clattering below. When they meet face-to-face, Valjean strikes the bishop, leaving him unconscious, and escapes with a heavy knapsack of silver.

The following morning, the bishop's wife laments the loss of her silver, but the bishop seems unperturbed, telling his wife, "So we'll use wooden spoons. I don't want to hear anything more about it." Moments later, authorities appear at the bishop's manor with the stolen silver and Valjean handcuffed.

Looking deeply into the thief's eyes, the bishop says, "I'm very angry with you, Jean Valjean." Turning toward the authorities, he asks, "Didn't he tell you he was our guest?"

"Oh, yes," replies the chief authority, "after we searched his knapsack and found all this silver. He claimed that you gave it to him."

Stooping in shame, Valjean expects the bishop to indict him. A new prison sentence awaits him. But the bishop says, "Yes. Of course, I gave him the silverware." Then, looking intently at Valjean, he asks, "But why didn't you take the candlesticks? That was very foolish. They're worth at least 2,000 francs. Why did you leave them? Did you forget to take them?"

The bishop orders his wife to hurry and fetch the candlesticks, while the authorities stand dumbfounded. They ask, "Are you saying he told us the truth?"

The bishop replies, "Of course. Thank you for bringing him back. I'm very relieved."

The authorities immediately release Valjean, who is shocked by the turn of events, and the bishop thrusts the retrieved candlesticks into Valjean's knapsack.

Once the authorities leave, the bishop drops the heavy bag of silver at Valjean's feet. After peeling away Valjean's hood, which was cloaking his guilty face, the bishop sternly looks him in the eyes and orders him, "Don't forget—don't ever forget—that you've promised to become a new man."

Valjean, trembling, makes the promise and with utter humility asks, "Why are you doing this?"

The bishop places his hands on Valjean's shoulders, as an act of blessing, and declares, "Jean Valjean, my brother, you no longer belong to evil. With this silver, I've bought your soul. I've ransomed you from fear and hatred. Now I give you back to God."

The Bible says in Romans 8:1, *There is therefore now no condemnation to those who are in Christ Jesus* (NKJV). In other words, you've been set free from any kind of condemnation because you have repented, made a change of behavior, of thoughts, and of your heart, and turned toward the things of God. The wonderful thing about repentance is that when you turn away from your sins, you no longer have to judge your life by the people around you; you only need to judge your life by the cross and the Word of God. A person turned toward God no longer looks at everybody else and measures what they deserve or don't deserve based on what everybody else is getting. Instead, they look toward Jesus and measure what they deserve or don't deserve based on what He did at Calvary.

True repentance is turning to God. It is turning away from your sins and back to Him. You must let God change your heart which includes your thoughts, mind, and attitude. When you get right with God, He will give you a new purpose and passion, and that is the beginning of a truly extraordinary life.

Extraordinary Word

Read and/or memorize the following Scripture passages, allowing them to transform your life.

▸ *"Now change your mind and attitude to God and turn to him so he can cleanse away your sins and send you wonderful times of refreshment from the presence of the Lord"* (Acts 3:19 TLB).

▸ *Do not conform any longer to the pattern of this world, but be transformed by the renewing of your mind. Then you will be able to test and approve what God's will is—his good, pleasing and perfect will* (Romans 12:2).

▸ *For as he thinks in his heart, so is he* (Proverbs 23:7 NKJV).

▸ *I pray also that the eyes of your heart may be enlightened in order that you may know the hope to which he has called you, the riches of his glorious inheritance in the saints* (Ephesians 1:18).

▸ *Above all else, guard your heart, for it is the wellspring of life* (Proverbs 4:23).

Extraordinary Focus

▸ What does true repentance involve?

▶ According to this definition, have you truly repented?

▶ How does godly repentance put you into the position of receiving blessings from God?

Extraordinary Action

Is there anything in your life today for which you need to repent? In a journal or notebook, list the changes you are willing to make to move into the extraordinary life that God has for you.

Often we change jobs, friends, and even spouses—when what we really need to change is ourselves.

LEO TOLSTOY

STEP 3
RENEWAL:

EXTRAORDINARY CHANGE

DEATH VALLEY MAY NO LONGER DESERVE ITS NAME. Normally the hottest and driest place in North America, in 2005 this desert area in California experienced the wettest year in a century. As a result, colorful wildflowers are in bloom. Vast fields of desert gold poppy, desert star, evening primrose, and phacelia have sprouted in the usually barren moonscape, which includes the lowest point in the Western Hemisphere.

Heavy rains resulted in disaster for other parts of California through flooding and mudslides. But the rainwater has brought the desert to life. Referring to the explosion of color, a spokesman for the Theodore Payne Foundation said, "2005 is a year likely to be remembered as the wildflower show of a lifetime."

Renewal, the springing to life of something that once appeared to be dead, can come in the most unlikely of places—Death Valley, California, for example, or through a work of God's Spirit in the human heart.

WE MUST RENEW OUR LIVES—OUR THINKING, OUR BEHAVIOR, OUR ATTITUDES— BEFORE WE CAN STEP INTO EVERYTHING THAT GOD HAS PLANNED FOR US.

Even though they are saved and are going to heaven, many Christians still don't live the extraordinary life that is theirs because of what Jesus did for them. In order to live this extraordinary life, we need to first have a *revelation* that the Bible offers us abundant life. In John 10:10, Jesus made it clear that this abundant life is for us today: *"A thief comes to steal and kill and destroy, but I came to give life—life in all its fullness"* (NCV). I love the way *The Message* Bible words it: *"A thief is only there to steal and kill and destroy. I came so they can have real and eternal life, more and better life than they ever dreamed of."*

After we receive the revelation of abundant life through Christ, then we need to make a change through *repentance* in order to position ourselves to receive the abundant life. The next step is that of *renewal:* We must renew our lives—our thinking, our behavior, our attitudes—before we can step into everything that God has planned for us.

According to Open Doors Ministry, Chinese government officials became so fed up with sky-high rates of crime, drug addiction, and sickness in the county of

Lancan Lahu, in the Yunnan province, that in the mid-1990s they turned for help to the only model citizens in the area: the Christians.

"We had to admit that the Lahu people were a dead loss because of their addiction to opium," confessed an official. "Their addiction makes them weak and sick. Then they would go to one of their 'priests,' who required animal sacrifices of such extravagance that the people became poor. And because they were so poor, they stole from each other, and law and order deteriorated. It was a vicious cycle that no amount of government propaganda could break.

"We noticed, however, that in some villages in the county, the Lahu were prosperous and peace-loving. There was no drug problem or any stealing or social order problems. Households had a plentiful supply of pigs, oxen, and chickens. So we commissioned a survey to find out why these villages were different. To our astonishment and embarrassment, we discovered the key factor was that these villages had a majority of Christians."

Officials launched a daring experiment in 1998, the likes of which would have been unthinkable in China ten years previously—they sponsored Christians to go into the troublesome villages and share their faith.

They started by picking out the worst village, which had 240 people, 107 of which were hopelessly addicted to opium. Christian Lahus were bussed into the village at government expense, and the villagers were herded together by the police and made to listen to the testimonies of the Christians.

A year later, there were seventeen converts in the village, and they began to grow more wealthy because they stopped spending their money on drugs. Eight of the seventeen converts even had enough to own sewing machines and start small businesses.

By early 2002, eighty-three of the villagers were Christians and the prosperity had spread. The government official said, "We are delighted with the results and have been extending the tactic to many other villages since then."[1]

Renewal—extraordinary change—is possible when we submit our lives to Christ, go where He sends us, and renew our hearts and minds in the process.

Renewing Your Mind

To renew our minds, we must first have an understanding of the Word of God. Just being a Christian or owning a Bible doesn't make us literate in the Word, just like owning a computer doesn't mean we understand the workings of a computer. But getting to know the Bible and allowing it to sink deep within our spirit will cause us to have a greater experience with God and bring about renewal in our hearts. Let's look at the words the apostle Paul wrote to his young protégé, Timothy, encouraging him to renew the faith that was inside of him.

Paul, an apostle of Christ Jesus by the will of God, according to the promise of life that is in Christ Jesus,

To Timothy, my dear son:

Grace, mercy and peace from God the Father and Christ Jesus our Lord.

I thank God, whom I serve, as my forefathers did, with a clear conscience, as night and day I constantly remember you in my prayers. Recalling your tears, I long to see you, so that I may be filled with joy. I have been reminded of your sincere faith, which first lived in your grandmother Lois and in your mother Eunice and, I am persuaded, now lives in you also. For this reason I remind you to **fan into flame the gift of God,** *which is in you through the laying on of my hands. For God did not give us a spirit of timidity, but a spirit of power, of love and of self-discipline.*

So do not be ashamed to testify about our Lord, or ashamed of me his prisoner. But join with me in suffering for the gospel, by the power of God.

2 Timothy 1:1–8, emphasis mine

Paul encouraged Timothy to "fan into flame," or renew, the gift of God that had been placed inside of him. A part of the Christian walk, if not most of it, is about keeping the faith alive in us. Paul said in 2 Timothy 4:7, *I have fought the good fight, I have finished the race, I have kept the faith.* The key to an extraordinary life is keeping the faith strong in spite of the difficulties and challenges that we face. But in order for us to keep the faith, we need to live a life of renewal so that we can get up every day—regardless of what is going on in our lives, whether we feel able or unable—and keep doing the things that God has called us to do.

A New Life

In the late 1920s, Jim and Betty Sullivan married and moved into Jim's old family home. It was a clapboard house with a hall down the middle. Betty was dissatisfied with the house, and so, in the 1930s, they decided to tear down the old house and build another to be their home for the rest of their lives.

WHEN GOD BRINGS US INTO HIS KINGDOM, THE OLD WAY OF LIVING MUST BE DISMANTLED AND DISCARDED.

Much to Betty's dismay, however, many of the materials of the old house were re-used in their new house. They used old facings and doors, and many other pieces of the finishing lumber. Everywhere that Betty looked, she saw that old house—old doors that wouldn't shut properly, crown molding split and riddled with nail holes, unfinished window trimming. It was a source of grief to her. For the rest of her life, she longed for a "new" house.

When God brings us into His kingdom, the old way of living must be dismantled and discarded. The *New Living Translation* of 2 Corinthians 5:17 reads this way: *What this means is that those who become Christians become new persons* [creatures]. *They are not the same anymore, for the old life is gone. A new life has begun!* In other words, we've just begun. When the old has gone, the new has come!

God wants us to stay in the race. God wants us to stay in the fight. God wants us to keep the faith! In order to do that, we need to live a renewed life, which begins with transformation. The Greek word translated as "transformed" is actually *metamorphoo*. Metamorphosis indicates a change—a transition in being, much like the change from the caterpillar to the cocoon to the butterfly. There is a process in our lives after we become Christians that causes us to become the person God created us to be. This process is renewal, and we must fully embrace the idea of renewal in order to begin living an extraordinary life.

> *Therefore, I urge you, brothers, in view of God's mercy, to offer your bodies as living sacrifices, holy and pleasing to God—this is your spiritual act of worship. Do not conform any longer to the pattern of this world, but be transformed by the renewing of your mind. Then you will be able to test and approve what God's will is—his good, pleasing and perfect will.*
>
> Romans 12:1–2

We are to be transformed by the renewing of our minds. In other words, we need to have a shift in our thinking—an internal shift in our lives. When that takes place, our lives will be transformed.

Are you willing to let God transform you? Are you ready to open yourself up to the "metamorphosis process" and let God become God in your life? Dig deep into His Word and let it begin to transform your thinking, your being, your circumstances—everything about you. Set up a time each day to read the Bible. Memorize the verses at the end of each chapter in this book. As you do, you will be amazed at how extraordinary your life can become!

Many Christians live very defensive lives. In other words, they are postured against the works of darkness, just waiting to be attacked. My friend, that is no way to live! Certainly we need to be aware of the devil and his tactics, but instead of waking up every morning in fear of the devil, we need to wake up every day and determine what God's plan and will is for us. When you begin to be transformed by the renewing of your mind, you no longer have to live your life in fear. Instead, you can live your life in faith, with the power of the Holy Spirit, and begin to move forward in the things of God.

The Five Principles of Renewal

So how should you go about gaining this renewal in your life? There are five basic biblical principles you must follow in order to cause this transformation to take place.

Be teachable.

First, you must **become teachable**. You must be willing to learn—but also remain humble in your knowledge. Jesus said, *"Take my yoke upon you and learn from me, for I am gentle and humble in heart, and you will find rest for your souls"* (Matthew 11:29).

Henry Augustus Rowland, professor of physics at Johns Hopkins University, was once called as an expert witness at a trial. During cross-examination, a lawyer demanded, "What are your qualifications as an expert witness in this case?"

The normally modest and retiring professor replied quietly, "I am the greatest living expert on the subject under discussion."

Later a friend well-acquainted with Professor Rowland's disposition expressed surprise at the professor's uncharacteristic answer.

To that, Rowland answered, "Well, what did you expect me to say? I was under oath!"

Knowledge is a great thing, but the Bible also tells us that *knowledge puffs up* (1 Corinthians 8:1), which is why we must practice humility in our learning.

There is a story I once heard of a teacher who was teaching a group of fifth graders. He looked around the room, and said, "Does anybody here understand electricity?" One rather anxious little boy named Jimmy, halfway down the middle aisle, pushed his hand up in the air and said, "I understand electricity!" The teacher looked at him and said, "Jimmy, would you please explain electricity to the class?" And he suddenly put his hand over his face and he said, "Oh, last night I knew, but this morning I've forgotten." The teacher, with tongue firmly planted in cheek, replied, "Now this is a tragedy. The only person in all of history who ever understood electricity and this morning he forgot it!"

READING THE WORD OF GOD WILL CHANGE YOUR LIFE.

Be teachable! Allow God to show you the things you need to know—and then learn them in humility. You'll be on your way to an extraordinary life.

Study the Word of God.

Secondly, when you begin to **learn the Word of God** and incorporate it into your circumstances, your life is refreshed. We are cleansed *by the washing with water through the word* (Ephesians 5:26). Reading the Word of God will change your life.

Half of the books of the Bible can be read in ten to forty-five minutes each, and many of them can be read in less than twenty. The entire Old and New Testaments can be read aloud slowly and with expression in less than seventy-one hours.

Wilber M. Smith wrote: "It will probably astonish many to know that one single, normal issue of *The Saturday Evening Post* contains as much reading matter as the entire New Testament. Thousands of people read *The Saturday Evening Post* through each week. The number of Christians who read the New Testament through every week, or even one whole book of the New Testament every week, are so few that we need not talk about it."[2]

King David loved the Lord, and he valued the words that God spoke, so much so that he wrote an entire psalm about it. In fact, this psalm is the longest chapter in the Bible—Psalm 119. Here are some verses from that psalm that express David's love for the Word—and what our love of the Scriptures should be like:

> *What you say goes, GOD,*
> *and stays, as permanent as the heavens.*
> *Your truth never goes out of fashion;*
> *it's as up-to-date as the earth when the sun comes*
> *up.*
> *Your Word and truth are dependable as ever;*
> *that's what you ordered—you set the earth going.*
> *If your revelation hadn't delighted me so,*
> *I would have given up when the hard times came.*
> *But I'll never forget the advice you gave me;*
> *you saved my life with those wise words.*
> *Save me! I'm all yours.*

I look high and low for your words of wisdom.
The wicked lie in ambush to destroy me,
but I'm only concerned with your plans for me.
I see the limits to everything human,
but the horizons can't contain your commands!
Oh, how I love all you've revealed;
I reverently ponder it all the day long.

PSALM 119:89-97 MSG

By your words I can see where I'm going;
they throw a beam of light on my dark path.
I've committed myself and I'll never turn back
from living by your righteous order.
Everything's falling apart on me, GOD;
put me together again with your Word.
Festoon me with your finest sayings, GOD;
teach me your holy rules.
My life is as close as my own hands,
but I don't forget what you have revealed.
The wicked do their best to throw me off track,
but I don't swerve an inch from your course.
I inherited your book on living; it's mine forever—
what a gift! And how happy it makes me!
I concentrate on doing exactly what you say—
I always have and always will.

PSALM 119:105-112 MSG

Mouth open and panting,
I wanted your commands more than anything....
My soul guards and keeps all your instructions—
oh, how much I love them!

PSALM 119:131,167 MSG

After passing through a period of skepticism, R. A. Torrey (1856–1928) yielded to Christ and studied in Germany. He was chosen in 1889 by D. L. Moody to oversee the fledgling Moody Bible Institute, and he also served as pastor of Moody Memorial Church. Between 1902 and 1906, he traveled around the world conducting evangelistic crusades with Charles M. Alexander, and from 1912 until 1924, he served as dean of the Bible Institute of Los Angeles (Biola)—all of this while speaking widely at Bible conferences and writing forty books.

His energy came from pouring himself into the Scriptures.

Once a man approached him, a Dr. Congdon, complaining that he could get nothing out of his Bible study. The Scripture seemed to be dry as dust. "Please tell me how to study it so that it will mean something to me."

"Read it," replied Dr. Torrey.

"I do read it."

"Read it some more."

"How?"

"Take some book and read it twelve times a day for a month."

"What book could I read that many times a day, working as many hours as I do?"

"Try Second Peter," replied Torrey.

The man later said, "My wife and I read Second Peter three or four times in the morning, two or three times at noon, and two or three times at dinner. Soon I was talking 'Second Peter' to everyone I met. It seemed as though the stars in the heavens were singing the story of 'Second Peter.' I read Second Peter on my knees, marking passages. Teardrops mingled with the ink colors, and I said to my wife, 'See how I have ruined this part of my Bible.'

"'Yes,' she said, 'but as the pages have been getting black, your life has been getting white.'"[3]

The water of the Word flows over our lives and begins to bring cleansing to the way we think and feel, to our pains, hurts, and rejection—whatever we have experienced, it brings cleansing to our souls.

So often people get born again, and they are so excited at that time because their sins have been washed away. They were lost and then they were found. The condemnation was removed from their lives. They were blind and then they could see. And in that moment, the brightness of God entered, and the passion for life began to burn—a God-experience that changed everything.

But then, over time, the value of that experience begins to wane unless the person visits that experience on a daily basis, several times throughout every day. At a garage sale, a friend of mine paid only one dollar for a ski bib that was worth at least $125. At one time, the original owner had wanted that ski bib badly enough to pay $125 for it, but by the time it was found in the garage sale, it was only worth one dollar to that same owner. If we're not careful, the great price that Jesus paid for us at the cross dwindles down to the mere statement: "I want to go to heaven." Yes, Jesus died to make it possible for us to spend eternity in heaven with Him, but He also died for so much more! He died so that you and I could live an extraordinary life *on this earth* here and now.

Use your talents for God.

The third aspect of renewal involves **the use of our talents** for the glory of God.

Aurlette was playing Christmas carols on the piano for her four-year-old great-granddaughter, Natalie. When she played, "Away in a Manger," Aurlette thought the child would enjoy hearing the words, so she started to sing as she played. After just a few words, she felt Natalie's hand on her arm, and as Aurlette looked down at her, she said, "Just let the piano sing it, Grandma."

> WHEN WE SERVE GOD WITH THE GIFTS HE HAS GIVEN TO US, IT REMINDS US OF THE PRICE THAT JESUS PAID FOR US.

Not all of us may be skilled at singing or playing the piano, but we *all* have been given a talent that we can use for the glory of God!

When we serve God with the gifts He has given to us, it reminds us of the price that Jesus paid for us. Jesus Himself said, *"The Son of Man did not come to be served, but to serve"* (Matthew 20:28). Jesus was giving us a model to follow: When we serve others, our lives will become extraordinary, and God will shower His blessings down upon us. When we serve God through our talents, it will bring a renewed sense of freshness to our purpose here on the earth. Something—that we don't always under-stand—happens when we serve others, but when we give of ourselves, we will see heaven opened and the miracles of God begin to take place in our lives.

In response to those who make excuses as to why they cannot serve the Lord, Rick Warren writes:

> Abraham was old, Jacob was insecure, Leah was unattractive, Joseph was abused, Moses stuttered, Gideon was poor, Samson was code-pendent, Rahab was immoral, David had an affair and all kinds of family problems, Elijah was suicidal, Jeremiah was depressed, Jonah was reluctant, Naomi was a widow, John the Baptist was eccentric to say the least, Peter was impulsive and hot-tempered, Martha worried a lot, the Samaritan woman had several failed marriages, Zacchaeus was unpopular, Thomas had doubts, Paul had poor health, and Timothy was timid. That is quite a variety of misfits, but

God used each of them in his service. He will use you too if you stop making excuses.[4]

Use the talents that God has given you! God is a creative God, and He gives each one of us unique talents. He gave Solomon wisdom and David the gift of praise; Aaron was an orator and Joseph interpreted dreams and became a ruler. He gave Abraham a promise, and the faith to believe it. He gave Jacob a new name, and made him into a great and mighty nation. He gave Esther beauty and courage, and through those gifts, she saved her people from destruction. The list is endless and each gift is unique. It has been said that between the great things we can't do and the little things we won't do, the danger is, we shall do nothing at all.

The Springfield, Oregon, public schools newsletter published an article that seems to be a parable of familiar frustration in the Body of Christ today.

Once upon a time, the animals decided they should do something meaningful to meet the problems of the new world. So they organized a school.

They adopted an activity curriculum of running, climbing, swimming, and flying. To make it easier to administer the curriculum, all the animals took all the subjects.

The *duck* was excellent in swimming, in fact, better than his instructor, but he made only passing grades in flying, and was very poor in running. Since he was slow in running, he had to drop swimming and stay after school to practice running. This caused his web feet to be badly worn, so that he was only average in swimming. But average was quite acceptable, so nobody worried about that—except the duck.

The *rabbit* started at the top of his class in running, but developed a nervous twitch in his leg muscles because of so much make-up work in swimming.

The *squirrel* was excellent in climbing, but he encountered constant frustration in flying class because his teacher made him start from the ground up instead of from the treetop down. He developed charley horses from overexertion, and so only got a C in climbing and a D in running.

The *eagle* was a problem child and was severely disciplined for being a nonconformist. In climbing classes he beat all the others to the top of the tree, but insisted on using his own way to get there.... [5]

The obvious moral of the story is a simple one: Each creature has its own set of capabilities in which it will naturally excel—unless it is expected or forced to fill a mold that doesn't fit. What is true of creatures in the forest is true of all of us in the Body of Christ. God has not made all of us the same. It's okay to be you … so relax! Enjoy your own capabilities, cultivate your own style. Appreciate the members of your church for who they are, even though their outlook or style may be miles different from yours. Rabbits don't fly. Eagles don't swim. Ducks look funny trying to climb. Squirrels don't have feathers. But you've got something to offer! Don't just get saved and then quit. Use your talents for the kingdom of God.

> WHEN WE OBEY GOD'S WORD AND BRING HIM THE TITHE, HE WILL BLESS US BEYOND WHAT WE COULD EVER EXPECT.

Tithe.

The fourth principle of renewal is that of the **tithe**. The Word of God says, *"Bring all the tithes into the storehouse, … And try Me now in this, … If I will not open for you the windows of heaven … And I will rebuke the devourer for your sakes"* (Malachi 3:10–11 NKJV). J. Oswald Sanders once said, "The basic question is not how much of *our* money we should give to God, but how much of *God's* money we should keep for ourselves." When we obey God's Word and bring Him the tithe, He will bless us beyond what we could ever expect. The *tithe* means "tenth." God only asks for one tenth of our income. Our renewal thinking recognizes that we can trust God with our finances. It represents our faith and trust in Him.

Charles Spurgeon once said, "Earn all you can, save all you can, and then give all you can. Never try to save out of God's cause; such money will canker the rest. Giving to

God is no loss; it is putting your substance into the best bank there is. Giving is true having, as the old gravestone said of the dead man, 'What I spent I had, what I saved I lost, what I gave I have.'"[6]

Cast all your cares on the Lord.

Finally, to truly experience renewal in our lives, we must **cast all of our cares upon Him.** When we have the Word of God embedded deep within our spirit, we know that everything in this world works together for good to those who are called according to His purpose (see Romans 8:28). First Peter 5:7 tells us, *Cast all your anxiety* [cares] *on him because he cares for you.*

Naturalist S. L. Bastian once told of a certain kind of spider that builds its nest in the branch of a small tree or bush. In this delicate enclosure the baby spiders are hatched. If the nest is disturbed in any way, the little spiders will all rush out in fright. At once, the mother goes to their side. She is alerted to their potential danger in a most unique manner. Each of the young ones has a thin, silky strand attached to it, and all of these threads are joined to the body of the mother. When the babies are threatened by an enemy, they naturally scurry off, giving their lines a sharp tug. This is instantly felt by the adult spider. Within seconds, she pulls them back to the nest where they are protected from harm.

The strands connecting the mother to the baby spiders calls to mind the work of Mary Slessor, missionary to Calabar, Nigeria. She would often rescue babies who were in danger and dying, and often the infants filled her home by the dozens. How to care for them through the night became a problem, especially when one of them stirred and cried. Mary learned to tie a string to each little hammock, lie in bed at night, and pull the strings as each baby needed soothing.

The prophet Hosea says that we are linked to God with cords of love, cords that cannot be broken (see Hosea 11:4). The gentle cords of His eternal love bind your heart to His. Tell the Lord, "God, I'm casting every care that I have upon You because You care for me. I'm not going to pay interest on tomorrow's troubles, but I'm going to transfer everything over to You, Lord, every day of my life."

The renewed life follows these five principles. Are you teachable? Are you involved in the study of God's Word? Do you use your talents for the glory of God? Do you practice bringing your tithes and offerings to the Lord? And do you release all of your anxiety to Him? A person living the transformed, renewed life understands that Jesus died, not just to allow us to go to heaven when we die, but to allow us to live extraordinary lives here on earth.

Extraordinary Word

Read and/or memorize the following Scripture passages, allowing them to transform your life.

▶ **Become teachable:** *Humble yourselves, therefore, under God's mighty hand that he may lift you up in due time* (1 Peter 5:6).

▶ **Study God's Word:** *Do not conform any longer to the pattern of this world, but be transformed by the renewing of your mind. Then you will be able to test and approve what God's will is—his good, pleasing and perfect will* (Romans 12:2).

▶ **Use your talents for God:** *Each one should use whatever gift he has received to serve others, faithfully administering God's grace in its various forms* (1 Peter 4:10).

▶ **Tithe:** *"Bring the whole tithe into the storehouse, that there may be food in my house. Test me in this," says the* LORD *Almighty, "and see if I will not throw open the floodgates of heaven and pour out so much blessing that you will not have room enough for it"* (Malachi 3:10).

▶ **Cast your anxiety:** *Cast all your anxiety on him because he cares for you* (1 Peter 5:7).

Extraordinary Focus

▸ How willing are you to allow God to transform your life? What obstacles are standing in the way?

▸ What talents has God given you to use in His service?

▸ How have you sought renewal—extraordinary change—in your own life?

Extraordinary Action

Consider the five principles of renewal and how they relate to your own life.

▸ Are you *teachable?* In what ways could you foster a more teachable spirit in your life?

▸ Are you *learning God's Word?* Make a commitment to the study and memorization of the Bible.

▸ Are you *using your talents?* Find out your spiritual gifts, the talents that God has given you personally, and find a way to use them in your local church.

▸ Are you *tithing?* If not, make the commitment to start today!

▸ Are you *casting your cares on Jesus?* What are your personal worries and concerns? In a journal or notebook, write a prayer to relinquish these things to the Lord.

Too often we underestimate the power of a touch, a smile, a kind word, a listening ear, an honest compliment, or the smallest act of caring: all of which have the potential to turn a life around.

LEO BUSCAGLIA

STEP 4
RELATIONSHIPS:

EXTRAORDINARY
CONNECTIONS

A MAN ONCE HAD A FINE CANARY WHOSE SONG WAS unusually beautiful. During the summer, it seemed a shame to keep the bird inside the house all the time. So the owner placed the cage in a nearby tree for the bird to enjoy the sunshine and the fresh air.

Many sparrows frequented the tree and were attracted to the cage. At first the canary was frightened, but soon he began to enjoy his companions. Gradually, and almost imperceptibly, he lost the sweetness of the song. By the end of the summer, his "singing" was little more than the twitter of the sparrows. Spending his summer in the wrong environment had caused the canary to lose his finest song.

God has called you to live an extraordinary life. You are that fine canary with a beautiful song to sing, but the relationships you foster will either make your song sweeter or they will transform your beautiful melody into meaningless twitter. You and I are, to a large degree, who we are today because of the people we have associated with in the past. Our associations are critical to our futures and our lives. Our relationships will either make us or break us, kill us or cause us to thrive.

GOD LONGS FOR A PASSIONATE RELATIONSHIP WITH YOU.

God has an extraordinary plan for your life woven into your very DNA. God has such phenomenal things planned that there is no way you will ever be able to comprehend them with your natural mind. The apostle Paul wrote:

> *And so here I am, preaching and writing about things that are way over my head, the inexhaustible riches and generosity of Christ. My task is to bring out in the open and make plain what God, who created all this in the first place, has been doing in secret and behind the scenes all along. Through Christians like yourselves gathered in churches, this extraordinary plan of God is becoming known and talked about even among the angels!*
>
> EPHESIANS 3:8–10 MSG

This extraordinary plan God has for you and me is so incredible that even the angels talk about it! For that very reason, it is important to ensure that the relationships we have in our lives will breathe life, not death, into the dreams and visions God has for us.

A Relationship with God

The first relationship that will help to bring about the dream God has for your life is your relationship with God Himself. This extraordinary relationship is the most critical of all, because it is the relationship that will release the power of heaven on your behalf to bring your dreams to pass. God longs for a passionate relationship with you. He needs a relationship with you, because He needs a heart through which to love. Without His love shining through you, it will never be reflected to the world. God needs a relationship with you because He needs a voice through which to speak His gospel. And He needs a relationship with you because He longs to use your hands to help the suffering and needy people of the world.

Someone once asked evangelist Dwight Moody how he managed to remain so intimate in his relationship with Christ. He replied, "I have come to know Him as the best friend I have ever found, and I can trust Him in that relationship. I have believed He is Savior; I have believed He is God; I have believed His atonement on the cross is mine, and I have come to Him and submitted myself on my knees, surrendered everything to Him, and gotten up and stood by His side as my friend, and there isn't any problem in my life, there isn't any uncertainty in my work, but I turn and speak to Him as naturally as to someone in the same room, and I have done it these years because I can trust Jesus."[1]

God is passionate about you and the plans that He has for your life! *For I know the plans I have for you, says the Lord. They are plans for good and not for evil, to give you a future and a hope* (Jeremiah 29:11 TLB). When you enter a relationship with Him, He will see to it that all of the plans He has for you, His purpose for your extraordinary life, will come to pass.

A Relationship with Others

In addition to a relationship with God, we need relationships with other people who will encourage us in the dreams and visions God gives to us. When God promised to meet the needs of His children, we can safely assume that includes our need for meaningful friendships. As we love Him and seek to love others, He will send to us those who can meet our needs for fellowship and intimacy.

In his book *To China with Love,* missionary J. Hudson Taylor told of being in Shanghai and feeling that the Lord wanted him to enter the Swatow region of China, an area rife with opium and slave trafficking without a single missionary there to preach the Gospel.

But Taylor didn't want to go, because he didn't want to leave his friend and mentor, Rev. William Burns, an English Presbyterian on whose friendship Taylor was depending for his spiritual and emotional well-being. He and Burns had become very close, and the thought of separation was more than Taylor could bear.

Then one day while taking afternoon tea at the American Presbyterian Mission House in Shanghai, a missionary sang a hymn entitled "The Missionary Call." The words spoke of being willing to give up friends and "every tie that binds the heart" for the sake of the kingdom of God. Taylor was deeply smitten, and that evening he invited his friend William Burns for a talk.

He says, "With many tears I told him how the Lord had been leading me, and how rebellious I had been and unwilling to leave him for this new sphere of labor. He listened with a strange look of surprise, and of pleasure rather than pain; and answered that he had determined that very night to tell me that he had heard the Lord's call to Swatow, and that his one regret had been the prospect of severance of our happy fellowship. We went together; and thus we recommenced missionary work in that part of China, which in later years has been so abundantly blessed."[2]

Most of us know the story of Elijah and Elisha. The great prophet Elijah anointed Elisha to succeed him in his ministry, but that wasn't the end of Elisha's preparation. Elisha spent time with Elijah, following him around, learning everything he could about the things of God.

Finally the time came for Elijah to leave the earth. When the fiery chariot came to take him to heaven, Elisha was right there, and Elijah's mantle fell to the ground. Elisha picked up the mantle and received twice the anointing that Elijah ever had. (See 2 Kings 2.)

Gordon MacDonald points out that the apostle Paul, as strong as he was, had a great need and a great capacity for friendship: "The apostle Paul was clearly a man committed to raising up a band of special friends. He knew who they were, and he regularly recognized them for their contribution to his spiritual passion. His friends were a resource upon which he obviously depended and without which he would not have survived. His address book of special friends would have included Aquila and Priscilla, with whom he occasionally worked and lived (see Acts 18:3), Onesiphorus ('for he oft refreshed me' 2 Tim. 1:16 KJV), Philemon ('I have derived much joy and comfort from your love' Philemon 1:7 RSV), Luke, and a host of others. Paul's friends came in all ages and backgrounds, and he seems to have taken great care to cultivate them."[3]

You and I will pick up what we're around. We will become like the people we associate with. So stay close to the anointing. Stay close to the favor of God. Stay close to those who demonstrate His power. David du Plessis, sometimes called "Mr. Pentecost," used to say, "Great men of God, I would seek them out." Seek out men and women of God who will plant great things into your life. People seldom improve when they have no other model but themselves to emulate. We need an extraordinary relationship with God and with other godly men and women in order to live the extraordinary life we are called to live.

A Relationship with the Church

Missionary James King tells the true story of an African woman in one of his churches who attended every service accompanied by an old, mongrel dog. He would enter with the lady and sit beside her during the service. She always sat on an outside seat beside the aisle. At the conclusion of the service, when the invitation was given, the woman would always come and kneel at that altar for prayer, and the dog would faithfully take his place beside her.

The woman's husband was a cruel man who deeply resented her devotion to Christ, and one day he beat her so severely that she died, and he even denied her a Christian funeral.

After the woman's death and burial, only the man and the dog were left. But he noticed that the dog disappeared on Wednesday evening about seven o'clock and didn't reappear for two hours. Every Sunday morning the dog likewise disappeared for a couple of hours.

GOD ESTABLISHED HIS CHURCH ON THIS EARTH TO ACCOMPLISH HIS WILL, NOT ONLY IN OUR INDIVIDUAL LIVES, BUT ALSO IN THE WORLD.

One Sunday, the man's curiosity was so aroused that he decided to follow and see where the dog went. Hurrying to keep up, the man followed the dog to the little church and watched as the dog took his seat on the aisle while the service went on. At the close of the service, the dog went to the altar and took his place where the wife had prayed.

The man was so touched in his spirit that he, too, went forward and gave his life to Christ. That woman's connection to her local church eventually led to her husband's salvation.

How vital to our extraordinary way of life is our relationship with the local church! God established His church on this earth to accomplish His will, not only in our individual lives, but also in the world. The church that I pastor will give between a half million and a million dollars this year to preach the gospel to the nations of the earth. The local church will minister to families in the hospital. The local church will minister in the prisons. The local church will influence the political process. The local church will make a difference in the world.

The first megachurch ever established was found on a hillside when Jesus preached to at least ten to twenty thousand people, including women and children. After He fed them spiritually, He also met their physical needs by multiplying the loaves and fishes for them to eat. He gave a model for the local church: We are to be about the business of feeding people spiritually, as well as meeting practical, physical needs in the community.

Hebrews 10:25 tells us, *Let us not neglect our meeting together, as some people do, but encourage and warn each other, especially now that the day of his coming back again is drawing near* (NLT). There is a legend of a village in Southern Europe that boasted of a church called "The House of Many Lamps." When it was built in the sixteenth century, the architect provided for no light except for a receptacle at every seat for the placing of a lamp. Each Sunday night, as the people gathered, they would bring their lanterns and slip them into the bracket at their seat. When someone stayed away, his place would be dark; and if very many stayed away, the darkness became greater for the whole. It was the regular presence of each person that lit up the church.

Unfortunately, the greatest deception of all is confronting the church of this generation. The tricky thing about deception is that it always has a measure of truth in it. Satan would like to come in and deceive the church today into dividing itself, into thinking that each individual local body can stand on its own, that we don't need the other members of the Body of Christ. What did Jesus say about a house divided against itself? He said: *"Every kingdom divided against itself will be ruined, and every city or household divided against itself will not stand. If Satan drives out Satan, he is divided against himself. How then can his kingdom stand? And if I drive out demons by Beelzebub, by whom do your people drive them out? … But if I drive out demons by the Spirit of God, then the kingdom of God has come upon you"* (Matthew 12:25-28). *The Message* Bible translates it like this: *"A family that's in a constant squabble disintegrates"* (verse 25). Later on, Jesus said, *"This is war, and there is no neutral ground. If you're not on my side, you're the enemy; if you're not helping, you're making things worse"* (verse 30, MSG).

Jesus was right: We *are* at war! Society is battling so strongly against the local church that one strategist has made some dire projections. In 2000, just seven years ago, 70 percent of all believers in the United States expressed their faith inside the environment of a local church. However, he predicts that by the year 2025, just twenty-five years later, only 30 to 35 percent of believers will give expression to their faith and experience inside of a local body. But here's the frightening part: In the year 2000, only 5 percent of believers expressed their faith in what is termed an "alternative faith-based community." That phrase indicates groups that have *left* the church, the Body of Christ, and become things like marketplace-ministry groups, home groups, etc. To be clear, these are not cell groups or extensions of a local church. These are groups of people who have decided to leave the authority of the church and go "do their own thing." And sadly, by the year 2025, it is predicted that 30 to 35 percent of *all believers* will choose to express their faith through one of these splinter groups.[4]

Now, there is a real danger in just "doing your own thing." God didn't call us to do our own thing. He calls us to come together, to come under the authority of the church, the Bride of Christ. According to Ephesians 4:11, [God] *gave some to be apostles, … prophets, … evangelists, … pastors and teachers* for the equipping of the saints. He gave these gifts to His church, not to some splinter group who just wants to go its own way.

Doesn't it make sense that the plan of the devil is to divide and conquer? Many of these people who have left the church have done so out of hurt or anger at what someone inside the church did to them. No, the Body of Christ is not perfect, and hurting people hurt people. But that is where the grace of the Lord Jesus comes in—as we learn to forgive one another and extend His mercy to our brothers and sisters.

The story is told of two porcupines in Northern Canada who were huddled together to get warm. But their quills pricked each other, so they moved apart. Before long they were shivering, so they sidled close again. Soon both were getting jabbed again. Same story; same ending. They need each other, but they kept needling each other.

Unthinkable and unnatural though it may seem, Jesus' Bride has had disagreements and quarrels for centuries. We tend to get along for a little while and then we are back at each other's throats. After a bit, we make up, walk in wonderful harmony for a short while, then we turn on one another again. We can switch from friend to fiend in a matter of moments. And God is grieved every time we do so. The only way the Body of Christ will be able to stand strong in this day and age is if we begin to work in unity with one another.

It reminds me of a "Peanuts" cartoon I once saw. In it, Lucy says to Snoopy, "There are times when you really bug me, but I must admit there are also times when I feel like giving you a big hug."

Snoopy replies, "That's the way I am … huggable and buggable."

We have been given an extraordinary purpose to reach a city, change a nation, and touch the world, but in order to fulfill that purpose, we must connect with our local church, those "huggable and buggable" brothers and sisters whom God has called to walk alongside of us.

A Relationship with the World

Not only must we have an extraordinary relationship with God, with others, and with the local church, but we also must have an extraordinary relationship with the world. This is where many churches miss the boat. They say, "We've got to separate ourselves from the world!" In one sense, they are right, because we do have a separate cause and a purpose that is different from the world. But you and I were never called to physically withdraw ourselves from the world. Jesus came to this earth and planted Himself right in the middle of a world that had no Christians in it! But He was enabled to reach the world because He had an extraordinary relationship with His Father that empowered Him to overcome the temptations and the trials of the world He had entered.

Vince Havner once said, "The Gospel is not something we come to church to hear; it is something we go from church to tell."[5] Charles Spurgeon said, "Our great object of glorifying God is to be mainly achieved by the winning of souls."[6] And Joseph Aldrich summarized, "God's evangelistic strategy in a nutshell: He desires to build into you and me the beauty of His own character, and then put us on display."[7]

Bill Bright said, "Although I have shared Christ personally with many thousands of people through the years, I am a rather reserved person and I do not always find it easy to witness.

"But I have made this my practice, and I urge you to do the same: Assume that whenever you are alone with another person for more than a few moments, you are there by divine appointment to explain to that person the love and forgiveness he can know through faith in Jesus Christ."[8]

Dr. Doren Edwards, a surgeon in Erin, Tennessee, tells of a patient of his, Blanche Bennet, whose alcoholic husband had died. Her two children were giving her problems, finances were tight, and life was very hard. She wasn't a Christian.

One day she came to see Dr. Edwards with physical problems, and he diagnosed her with cancer; multiple organs were involved. No treatment was available, and she was very bitter. Dr. Edwards, a Christian and a Gideon, wanted to talk with her about the Lord, but she wouldn't allow him to share his witness. She did, however, accept a small New Testament.

A few weeks later, the doctor learned from the newspaper obituary that she had died. He sent a card to the family, telling them that he had donated Bibles in her memory to the Gideons.

THE BIBLE TELLS US VERY SPECIFICALLY TO GO INTO ALL THE WORLD— INTO EVERY NATION—AND TO MAKE DISCIPLES OF ALL PEOPLE.

The woman's daughter called him. "Could you please send us a Bible like the ones you donated in memory of our mother?" she asked. "We don't have a Bible in our home. The last six days she was alive, her whole life changed. She was no longer bitter, she wasn't afraid to die, and she said something about knowing Jesus. But she asked that her Bible be buried in her hand, and so we couldn't keep it. Would you please send us a Bible so that we can find what Mama found in that book?"

Dr. Edwards sent them a Bible, and to date, the daughter, the son, and one sister have been saved as a result.

The evangelistic harvest is always urgent. The destiny of men and of nations is always being decided. Every generation is strategic. We are not responsible for the past generation, and we cannot bear the full responsibility for the next one; but we do have our generation. God will hold us responsible as to how well we fulfill our responsibilities to this age and take advantage of the opportunities that have been given to us.

The best evangelistic center in the greater metropolitan Boston area is not a church. It is a filling station in

Arlington. It was owned and operated by a man named Bob who caught the vision early in his life that his vocation and his calling were to be welded together. As time passed, his station became known as the place to go for gas, new tires, or other car service. There have been a half-dozen cars lined up bumper to bumper near two pumps in front of that little station just waiting to be served by that man. He has no banners out, no "Jesus Saves" flags, no signs, no "ichthuses," nothing plastered all over the station or in the windows, no sign, "Bring your car to Bob and take your soul to Jesus." He simply *did his job!* He did it well, and people knew he was in partnership with the Lord. He led dozens of people to faith in Jesus Christ.

The Bible tells us very specifically to go into all the world—into every nation—and to make disciples of all people. I love the way Saint Francis of Assisi said it: "Preach the gospel of Jesus Christ wherever you go, and if necessary, use words." Don't be afraid of the world! If you have an extraordinary relationship with God, if you have an extraordinary relationship with other believers, and if you are part of an extraordinary, life-giving church, then you will be able to be a light shining in the darkness of a lost and dying world.

Extraordinary relationships. A friend of mine once said: "You cannot touch your neighbor's heart with anything less than your own." Extraordinary relationships will lead to an extraordinary life.

Extraordinary Word

Read and/or memorize the following Scripture passages, allowing them to transform your life.

▸ *For I know the plans I have for you, says the Lord. They are plans for good and not for evil, to give you a future and a hope* (Jeremiah 29:11 TLB).

▸ *But if we walk in the light, as he is in the light, we have fellowship with one another, and the blood of Jesus, his Son, purifies us from all sin* (1 John 1:7).

▸ *Iron sharpens iron; so a man sharpens the countenance of his friend [to show rage or worthy purpose]* (Proverbs 27:17 AMP).

▸ *Let us not neglect our meeting together, as some people do, but encourage and warn each other, especially now that the day of his coming back again is drawing near* (Hebrews 10:25 NLT).

▸ Jesus said, *"Therefore go and make disciples of all nations, baptizing them in the name of the Father and of the Son and of the Holy Spirit, and teaching them to obey everything I have commanded you. And surely I am with you always, to the very end of the age"* (Matthew 28:19-20).

▸ Jesus said, *"For I was hungry and you gave me something to eat, I was thirsty and you gave me something to drink, I was a stranger and you invited me in, I needed clothes and you clothed me, I was sick and you looked after me, I was in prison and you came to visit me. ... I tell you the truth, whatever you did for one of the least of these brothers of mine, you did for me"* (Matthew 25:35-36, 40). (For further study, read the entire parable of the sheep and the goats in Matthew 25:31-46.)

Extraordinary Focus

▸ How is your relationship with God? What are some ways you might strengthen it this week?

▸ How are your relationships with other people? Do you have godly friendships in your life that increase your faith, or are your relationships tearing you down? How can you become a better friend?

▸ Are you a part of a Bible-believing, life-giving active local church? If not, how can you make such a church a part of your life? If so, how can you become more involved?

▸ Are you an active witness for the Lord Jesus Christ? If not, what is holding you back? If so, what difference has it made in your life?

Extraordinary Action

How will you improve your relationships...

▸ with God?
▸ with others?
▸ with the church?
▸ with the world?

*The best discipline,
maybe the only
discipline that really
works, is self-discipline.*

WALTER KIECHEL III

STEP 5
ROUTINES:

EXTRAORDINARY DISCIPLINE

PLAYERS GATHERING FOR THE FIRST DAY OF basketball practice at UCLA were full of antici-pation. They wondered how their coach, John Wooden, would set the tone for the long season to come. They didn't have to wait long.

Veterans knew what was coming. But first-year players were no doubt perplexed by the initial lesson imparted by their Hall of Fame coach: He taught them how to put on a pair of socks. He did not teach this lesson only once, but before every game and practice. Why?

Wooden had discovered that many players didn't prop-erly smooth out the wrinkles in the socks around their heels and little toes. If left uncorrected, these wrinkles could cause blisters that could hamper their performance at crucial times during games. Many players thought that the practice was odd and laughed about it at the time. Wooden knows that some of them still laugh about it even today. But the coach would not compromise on this basic fundamental principle.

In our desire to grow as Christians, we can easily forget about the fundamentals of our faith. But if we do, we run the risk of developing painful spiritual blisters that can hurt us as we run our race. Spiritual routines are important to keep us "in the game," on the way toward the life that God has for us.

To most people, routines indicate boring tasks of drudgery, performed without any excitement or fulfillment. But that isn't how God meant for us to live! He wants to take our routines—the things we do in our everyday lives—and use them to accomplish His destiny for us. The Bible says, *Let us not become weary in doing good, for at the proper time we will reap a harvest if we do not give up* (Galatians 6:9).

To live an extraordinary life, we first need a *revelation* of what He has done for us, and then we must *repent* by turning away from ordinary lives and turning to an extraordinary God. We must *renew* our minds and our hearts by the power of the Holy Spirit. And then we must foster new *relationships* that will make us better than we ever would have been without them.

Once that has been accomplished, we must establish new extraordinary *routines* that will cause our lives to change. When we create habits in our lives, then our habits define who we are. In other words, if you and I will establish new routines in our lives, we won't need to worry about yesterday's problems because we will be looking toward the future. Romans 4:17 tells us, *God ... speaks of future events with as much certainty as though they were already past* (TLB). Sometimes we need to declare things that may not be as though they already were—and watch God move by the faith that we are releasing out of our mouths.

In his book *Teaching the Elephant to Dance*, James Belasco describes how trainers shackle young elephants with heavy chains to deeply embedded stakes. In that way, the elephant learns to stay in its place. Older, powerful elephants never try to leave—even though they have the strength to pull up the stake and walk away. Their conditioning has limited their movements. With only a small metal bracelet around their foot attached to nothing, they stand in place. The stakes are actually gone!

> WE TURN TOWARD JESUS, THE LORD OF OUR LIVES, AND WHEN WE STAY FOCUSED ON HIM, WE BEGIN TO DEVELOP NEW HABITS

Like powerful elephants, many people are bound by earlier conditioned restraints. Yet when the circus tent catches on fire and the elephant sees the flames and smells the smoke, it forgets its old conditioning and runs for its life![1]

Most Christians spend their whole lives looking back at all the things they used to do—and trying not to do those things again. They aren't looking ahead to all the things that God has for their future. When you get born again, it's not time to deal with your past; it's time for you to face God and let Him deal with your past. It's time to say, "I'm not looking at my past. I'm going to establish new routines that are going to bring the extraordinary into my life." We've all got a "yesterday," but the yesterday we have is no longer the god of our lives once we've given it all to Jesus. We turn toward Jesus, the Lord of our lives, and when we stay focused on Him, we begin to develop new habits.

On June 1, 2003, twenty-one-year-old rookie police officer Jeff Postell from Murphy, North Carolina, on routine patrol, did what hundreds of FBI and other law-enforcement officers had not: He arrested one of the nation's most wanted fugitives, Eric Robert Rudolph, suspected in the bombing at Olympic Park in Atlanta, Georgia, in 1996.

Officer Postell was working an overnight shift when he spotted a suspicious man crouching in the middle of an alley behind a shopping center. Originally, Rudolph gave him a phony name. Later, he admitted to his real name. Officer Postell thought at first that he had just nabbed a run-of-the-mill prowler. Only later did he discover Rudolph's notoriety.

"I was just doing what I was supposed to be doing," said the young officer. "That's just in a day's work."[2]

Life is best lived with a routine. As followers of Jesus Christ, a faithful routine of prayer and praise, Scripture reading and study, and tithing and giving to others, is essential. The hit-and-miss approach won't lead to a fulfilled life.

The Message Bible describes a group of people who established habits that were extraordinary.

> *Do you see what this means—all these pioneers who blazed the way, all these veterans cheering us on? It means we'd better get on with it. Strip down, start running—and never quit! No extra spiritual fat, no parasitic sins. Keep your eyes on Jesus, who both began and finished this race we're in. Study how he did it. Because he never lost sight of where he was headed—that exhilarating finish in and with God—he could put up with anything along the way: cross, shame, whatever. And now he's there, in the place of honor, right alongside God. When you find yourselves flagging in your faith, go over that story again, item by item, that long litany of hostility he plowed through. That will shoot adrenaline into your souls!*
>
> *In this all-out match against sin, others have suffered far worse than you, to say nothing of what Jesus went through—all that bloodshed! So don't feel sorry for yourselves. Or have you forgotten how good parents treat children, and that God regards you as his children?*

My dear child, don't shrug off God's discipline,
but don't be crushed by it either.
It's the child he loves that he disciplines;
the child he embraces, he also corrects.

God is educating you; that's why you must never
drop out. He's treating you as dear children. This
trouble you're in isn't punishment; it's training,
the normal experience of children. Only irrespon-
sible parents leave children to fend for themselves.
Would you prefer an irresponsible God? We respect
our own parents for training and not spoiling us,
so why not embrace God's training so we can truly
live?

HEBREWS 12:1-9

You see, one routine is overcome by another. This great cloud of witnesses stuck together and encouraged one another. Once you get the idea that you are going to start a new routine and stick with it, you will encounter people who will help you out in your perseverance.

Two men went out to play golf, and one of them said to the other, "That's the tenth time I've swung at that ball, and I still haven't hit it!" His friend replied, "Well, keep swinging. I think you've got it worried."

Sometimes we need someone to breathe life onto our new routines and say, "Don't you ever give up!" Fortunately, God has blessed us with a great cloud of witnesses, and they are continually encouraging us: "Keep on swinging!

I think you've got the devil worried. Keep on walking it out—I think he's scared. Keep on believing—I think he's shaking in his boots!"

Don't you dare quit! Don't you dare stop doing the things that God has called you to do! It's only the beginning of the great things ahead that your heavenly Father has planned for you. There is a grand coliseum in heaven that is packed to capacity today with the great saints of the past, and they are looking down upon God's people in the earth and encouraging us to win. They are cheering us on, saying, "If you'll just keep running, if you'll just keep believing, and if you'll just keep declaring the victory—then nothing will be too difficult for you. We've been there. We know!"

> THE FIRST THING THAT MUST HAPPEN WHEN YOU ARE ESTABLISHING A NEW ROUTINE OR HABIT IS *CONSISTENCY.*

There are four qualities that you must have in order to successfully implement new routines into your life: *consistency, resistance, persistence,* and *assistance.*

Consistency

Good, better, best; never let it rest—until your good is better and your better is your best!
DAISY HEPBURN

Bad habits, or negative routines, can bring personal embarrassment and physical limitations. American educator Horace Mann once described the predicament this way: "Habit is a cable; we weave a thread of it every day, and at last, we cannot break it."[3] Lloyd Cory said, "The chains of habit are too weak to be felt until they are too strong to be broken."[4] The first thing that must happen when you are establishing a new routine or habit is *consistency*. Notice I did not say *perfection*! So many times, the church sets people up for failure by expecting new believers to achieve perfection immediately. We bring people in, get them saved, and expect that all of their previous bad behavior will just disappear. Most of the time, it doesn't happen that way. Most of the time, people need to establish new routines that they begin to practice consistently, and by doing so, they will see their lives begin to change. Experts say that it takes twenty-one days to form a new habit—twenty-one days of practicing consistent good behavior—to cause a permanent change to take place. John Dryden said, "We first make our habits, and then our habits make us.[5]

As a seminarian, Gordon MacDonald was asked to write and deliver a paper to a special forum of students and faculty. Typical as it was for many seminary students, he put off writing the paper until the deadline loomed and then cut two days of classes to complete the assignment. On the day of his presentation, when he had finished reading the paper and the audience had responded with applause and left the auditorium, a professor whose classes

Gordon had dodged in order to write the paper found him and said, "Gordon, that was a good paper, but it lacked the possibility of greatness. Do you want to know why?"

Gordon MacDonald could hardly say no, and so the man continued. "You sacrificed your routine responsibilities to write it," he said. "Your ministry will not be successful if you make this sort of thing a habit."

You listen carefully to an insight like that when it comes from a man forty years your senior whom you respect. He was less interested in the content of Gordon's presentation than he was the character pattern that framed its writing. The paper would soon be forgotten, but the work habits it revealed would have continued for the rest of Gordon's life if he didn't alter them.

The professor saw this; Gordon had not. But the rebuke caused him to reform his work ethic and allowed Gordon MacDonald to become one of the premier theologians of our time.

Consistency, not perfection, will keep us doing the things that we know we ought to be doing, establishing habits that we ought to be establishing. Consistency allows us to be prepared for anything. Louis Pasteur said: "Chance favors the prepared mind."[6] Consistency in new and godly routines allows you to be ready for the opportunities that God will bring your way.

Resistance

The second thing that is necessary when establishing new routines is *resistance*. Resistance is not possible without submission to God. James 4:7 tells us, *Submit yourselves, then, to God. Resist the devil, and he will flee from you.* Until you submit to God, you will have no power to resist. But when you submit to Him and His will, you fill yourself with the power and the strength you need to resist anything the devil throws at you.

The trouble is, most people don't know how to live an extraordinary life because they don't know how to submit to God and to the people He places in their lives. Many people think of submission as an old-fashioned, outdated principle not to be considered in the twenty-first century. But that's not what the Bible tells us in James 4:7. We all must find someone to whom we can submit. Submit to God. Submit to your spouse. Submit to the teachings of your church. Submit to the godly authority in your life. Once you have true submission in place in your life, the power of God will be released to resist the devil and all of the schemes he wants to bring to pass. It will help you to resist the cravings of this world that could ultimately lead to your destruction and the destruction of the purposes God has for you.

Potato chips, cheese curls, and candy may be some of your favorite things to eat, but for a few mule deer in Arizona's Grand Canyon National Park, these foods proved to be deadly. Park rangers had to kill over two dozen mule deer because they became hooked on junk food left by visitors to the park.

Once they get a taste of the sugar and salt, the deer develop an extreme addiction and will go to any lengths to eat only junk food. The result is that the animals ignore the food they need, leaving them in poor health and on the edge of starvation. Because of junk food cravings, the deer lose their natural ability to digest vegetation. One park ranger called the junk food "the crack cocaine of the deer world."

The Scriptures warn us of the dangers of developing a craving for the things of this world. Such a diet keeps us from hungering for the things of God. We need to learn to develop resistance against such temptations and the works of the enemy.

The human body is a great example of how resistance works. Do you realize that God made the body so that it would heal itself? If you have established healthy routines in your life—if you're getting your rest, eating right, and exercising—your body will establish a strong immune system that will be able to resist viruses and disease. Why? Because you are submitted to a consistent routine that brings health to your body. There are exceptions, but as a rule, if you treat your body well, it will treat you well.

It's the same thing in the spiritual realm. When you have submitted to the healthy routines of daily Bible reading, prayer, and attending church, your mind will be renewed. And with a renewed mind comes the strength to resist the "viruses" of temptation and sin. Stay healthy! And let the power of God work in your life.

Persistence

Oliver Wendell Holmes wrote, "Every calling is great when greatly pursued."[7] The routines that will bring you to an extraordinary life will not always be easy to maintain. From time to time, you may grow fatigued, and you will have to say, "I know I have consistent routines that will bring me into the extraordinary life God has for me. I know I am submitted to God, and I am resisting the devil. I am becoming fatigued, but I will not quit! I will persist in doing the things that I know I should do." Persistence pays off! Persistence is obstinate determination. Our persistence places value on God's call on our lives.

OUR PERSISTENCE PLACES VALUE ON GOD'S CALL ON OUR LIVES.

We must never forget that the word *persevere* comes from the prefix *per,* meaning *through,* coupled with the word *severe*. It means to keep pressing on, to keep trusting God, looking up, doing our duty—even through "severe" circumstances.

In the thirteenth century, there was a disagreement between Scottish leaders about which of them should be king. England's King Edward I stepped in and took the honor for himself, stripping Scotland of its crown, its royal regalia, and even the sacred Stone of Scone on which the kings of Scotland had always been crowned. The latter he placed in Westminster Abbey in London.

The outraged Scots secretly crowned Robert Bruce their king, but they seemed no match for the English army. Scottish troops were scattered, living in the mountains, living on eels and salmon and deer, and under constant attack from their enemy. Robert Bruce himself was wounded, and his capture seemed imminent. The English had even captured one of his bloodhounds and were using it to search for him.

After madly careening through the Scottish woods, exhausted, frightened, and bleeding, Bruce suddenly came to a stream. Plunging in, he waded alongside the bank until hoisting himself onto the limb of a tree. There he stayed, and the dog lost the scent.

Bruce spent the ensuing winter hidden away in a hovel in the mountains, keeping himself alive on a bag of old potatoes. One cold, gray afternoon, he felt almost hopeless, his spirits badly draining. But then he noticed a spider trying to weave a web in the corner of the window. The creature was having a hard time of it, because the wind kept blowing away its threads. Time after time, the spider gave another effort until finally the thread held.

"I might be that spider," said Bruce. "I, too, have failed. Like those threads, my lines have been broken and blown away. But you have shown me that there is always one more time—a time for one more attempt and, with persistence, a winning one!"

Bruce left the hovel to gather his scattered troops, and by the springtime, he had an army that was tougher than ever. Battle after battle raged until their lines finally held and they drove the English out of Scotland. And the final, most interesting part of the story? Ever since that time, it is said, no one by the name of Bruce has ever killed a spider.

On October 29, 1941, Winston Churchill gave an address at Harrow School in Great Britain. He got up, went to the podium, and said, "Never give in, never give in, never, never, never, never—in nothing, great or small, large or petty—never give in except to convictions of honor and good sense. Never give in."[8] And then he left the podium and sat back down.

Your *persistence* places value on God's call on your life. You've been bought with a price. You've been covered by the blood of Christ. And so you must take up your cross daily and follow Him, not moved by discomfort, inconvenience, adversity, or opposition. You must persist in order to live the extraordinary life that God has for you.

Assistance

The truth is, we won't make it in this life without each other to lean on. *Two are better than one. ...A cord of three strands is not quickly broken* (Ecclesiastes 4:9,12). *As iron sharpens iron, so one man sharpens another* (Proverbs 27:17). We need *assistance* in the journey to extraordinary living. I don't always like what my wife has to say, but I know that she's called alongside me and I'm called alongside her. We're called to assist each other in the journey. We all need other people speaking into our lives.

Dr. Julius Segal, the distinguished psychologist who worked with the Iran hostages, Vietnam POWs, and other survivors, wrote a book entitled *Winning Life's Toughest Battles* in which he shared his observations of those who had overcome terrible traumas in their lives. His first chapter is devoted to the importance of having friends, a circle of comrades with whom to communicate. He wrote, "Few individuals can cope with trauma alone. Even the most powerful figures in the world need contact with others in the face of crisis."

He related the experience of Vice Admiral James B. Stockdale, heroic survivor of 2,714 days as a POW in Vietnam:

> On one occasion, the North Vietnamese hand-cuffed Stockdale's hands behind his back, locked his legs in heavy irons, and dragged him from his dark prison cell to sit in an unshaded court-yard so other prisoners could see what happened to anybody who refused to cooperate.
>
> Stockdale remained in that position for three days. Since he had not been in the sun for a long time, he soon felt weak, but the guards would not let him sleep. He was beaten repeatedly. After one beating, Stockdale heard a

towel snapping out in a prison code the letters: GBUJS. It was a message he would never forget: "God bless you, Jim Stockdale."

In every episode of captivity in recent American history, POWs and hostages have been sustained by ingeniously improvised life-lines of communication. In Vietnam, a clever tap code, in which the number and sequence of taps spelled out letters of the alphabet, became the prisoners' chief means of communication. It was this code that sustained Jim Stockdale.

At first the prisoners had trouble remembering the letter codes long enough to put them together to form coherent messages. Soon, however, their proficiency improved, and the system became second nature. The lonely prisoners tapped on the walls, the ceilings, or the floor. …

Eventually the POWs developed sophisticated extensions of the tapping routine. An especially effective ploy was to sweep through a prison compound using the broom movement to "talk" to an entire group. If one man walked by another's cell, he could drag his sandals in code. Some men sent messages to their comrades through the noises they made while shaking out their blankets, others by belching or blowing their noses. One POW feigned sleep for a couple of hours each day during the siesta period and through his snoring managed to report how everyone was doing and what was going on in his cellblock.[9]

Segal quotes former POW Everett Alvarez who later said, "We really got to know each other through our silent conversations across the brick walls. Eventually, we learned all about each other's childhood, background, experiences, wives and children, hopes and ambitions." Segal goes on to report a study of over two thousand people who had suffered trauma, including physical abuse, rape, or the death of a loved one. Survivors were healthier if they managed to confide in someone about the event. Those who hadn't discussed their experiences developed more illness of various sorts—from headaches to lung disease.[10]

> ROUTINES MAY SEEM MUNDANE, BUT IN ACTUALITY, THEY ARE THE VEHICLE THAT GOD OFTEN CHOOSES TO USE TO LEAD US INTO EXTRAORDINARY LIVES.

As you begin to excel in your extraordinary routines, you're never going to stop needing other people. You need them to help you develop the consistency, the resistance, and the persistence that it takes to follow the routines that will lead you to an extraordinary life.

One interesting scene in *The Passion of the Christ* shows Jesus finishing a table. In it, Jesus is depicted as having a commitment to putting out an excellent product. As a carpenter, He spent many long hours and years doing manual work in a wood shop. His work had to be of the highest quality.

The Christian apologist Justin Martyr made a revealing observation about Jesus' work. During Justin Martyr's life in second-century Galilee, he saw farmers still using plows made by Jesus. Theologian Os Guiness writes, "How intriguing to think of Jesus' plow in addition to His Cross—to wonder what it was that made His plows and yokes last and stand out."[11]

As Christians, we sometimes tend to exalt "spiritual" work—the "great things" God has called us to do. We often downplay the simple routines and persistent labor that will get us to those "great things." However, any work, any routine practice that God calls us to do, no matter how mundane, when it is done to the glory of God, will bring a great reward.

Routines may seem mundane, but in actuality, they are the vehicle that God often chooses to use to lead us into extraordinary lives. Let go of your past. Leave it behind you, and press forward to the things God has waiting for you. Philippians 3:13b says, ...*Forgetting what is behind and straining toward what is ahead.* Begin to establish new routines, new patterns of living, new ways of thinking and doing things. *"Behold, I will do a new thing,"* says the LORD (Isaiah 43:19 NKJV). Get on board with God's "new thing" today!

Extraordinary Word

Read and/or memorize the following Scripture passages, allowing them to transform your life.

▸ *Let us not become weary in doing good, for at the proper time we will reap a harvest if we do not give up* (Galatians 6:9).

▸ *Submit yourselves, then, to God. Resist the devil, and he will flee from you. Come near to God and he will come near to you. Wash your hands, you sinners, and purify your hearts, you double-minded* (James 4:7-8).

▸ *God is educating you; that's why you must never drop out. He's treating you as dear children. This trouble you're in isn't punishment; it's* training, *the normal experience of children. Only irresponsible parents leave children to fend for themselves. Would you prefer an irresponsible God? We respect our own parents for training and not spoiling us, so why not embrace God's training so we can truly* live? (Hebrews 12:8–9 MSG).

▸ *Not that I have already obtained all this, or have already been made perfect, but I press on to take hold of that for which Christ Jesus took hold of me. Brothers, I do not consider myself yet to have taken hold of it. But one thing I do: Forgetting what is behind and straining toward what is ahead, I press on toward the goal to win the prize for which God has called me heavenward in Christ Jesus* (Philippians 3:12–14).

▸ *"Behold, I will do a new thing,"* [says the Lord] (Isaiah 43:19 NKJV).

Extraordinary Focus

▸ What routines are currently in your life that are leading you to the extraordinary plans that God has for you?

▸ What routines are holding you back? How can you change those routines?

▸ How can you incorporate more *consistency, resistance, persistence,* and *assistance* in your spiritual routines?

Extraordinary Action

List five new routines that you could begin implementing into your life right away that will help to bring you into a new, extraordinary life

*To have a right to
do a thing is not at
all the same as to be
right in doing it.*

G. K. CHESTERTON

STEP 6
RIGHTEOUSNESS:

EXTRAORDINARY DECENCY

A sign in a coffee shop once read, "If you can start the day without caffeine; if you can get going without pep pills; if you can always be cheerful, ignoring aches and pains; if you can resist complaining and boring people with your troubles; if you can eat the same food every day and be grateful for it; if you can understand when your loved ones are too busy to give you any time; if you can overlook it when those you love take it out on you when through no fault of yours something goes wrong; if you can take criticism and blame without resentment; if you can ignore a friend's limited education and never correct him; if you can resist treating a rich man better than a poor man; if you can face the world without lies and deceit; if you can conquer tension without medical help; if you can relax without liquor; if you can sleep without the aid of drugs; if you

RIGHTEOUSNESS
EMPOWERS US
TO CONFORM
TO THE
MORALITY AND
THE PROPRIETY
OF THE WORD
OF GOD!

can say honestly that deep in your heart you have no prejudice against creed, color, religion, or politics; then, my friend, you are almost as good as your dog!"

What does it mean to be "good"? What does it mean to be "righteous"? There is no such thing as an extraordinary life without the righteousness of God. It is possible to be saved and have righteousness deposited in your heart, but have that righteousness lie dormant in your everyday life. But to truly live the extraordinary life that God has in store for you, you must awaken to righteousness! You must come alive to right living, living according to the standards that God has set.

I define *righteousness* as "extraordinary decency." Wouldn't it be wonderful if everyone in the world were decent and kind all of the time? The word *decency* means "conforming to standards of propriety and morality." The word *propriety* means "conforming to what is acceptable in conduct or speech." Righteousness empowers us to conform to the morality and the propriety of the Word of God! But we have to *activate* righteousness in our lives. We have to be sure that we're on the right track and that we are living life according to the will and plan of God.

In the book entitled *Actions Speak Louder Than Verbs*, Herb Miller writes:

> Two Kentucky farmers who owned racing stables had developed a keen rivalry. One spring, each of them entered a horse in a local steeple chase. Thinking that a professional rider might help him outdo his friend, one of the farmers engaged a crack jockey. The two horses were leading the race at the last fence, but it proved too tough for them. Both horses fell, unseating their riders. But this calamity did not stop the professional jockey. He quickly remounted and won the race.
>
> Returning triumphant to the paddock, the jockey found the farmer who had hired him fuming with rage. "What's the matter?" the jockey asked. "I won, didn't I?"
>
> "Oh, yes," roared the farmer. "You won all right, but you still don't know, do you?"
>
> "Know what?" asked the jockey.
>
> "You won the race on the wrong horse."[1]

You and I can have all kinds of success in our lives, but if we are not right with God in the process, it's meaningless. We may win the race according to the world's standards, but if we haven't pleased the Lord, we have not lived an extraordinary life. In a world that is filled with the misguided goals of maintaining our popularity and achieving a certain measure of success, sometimes we find it very difficult to continue on the right path, to stay on the "right horse," when we feel as if someone else is getting ahead of us. It's difficult to stay on the right path when we've been "thrown"—maybe not off of a horse, but thrown by a layoff, thrown by a spouse, thrown by our kids not behaving the way they should.

We need *God's* sense of righteousness, not our own. It's easy to try to live life by our own set of rules rather than God's, but that is not the path to an extraordinary life.

An armed robber named Dennis Lee Curtis was arrested in 1992 in Rapid City, South Dakota. Curtis apparently had scruples about his thievery. In his wallet, the police found a sheet of paper on which was written the following code:

1. I will not kill anyone unless I have to.
2. I will take cash and food stamps—no checks.
3. I will rob only at night.
4. I will not wear a mask.
5. I will not rob mini-marts or 7-Eleven stores.
6. If I get chased by the cops on foot, I will get away. If chased by vehicle, I will not put the lives of innocent civilians on the line.
7. I will rob only seven months of the year.
8. I will enjoy robbing from the rich to give to the poor.

This thief had a sense of morality, but it was flawed. When he stood before the court, he was not judged by the standards he had set for himself, but by the higher law of the state. Likewise, when we stand before God, we will not be judged by the code of morality that we have written for ourselves, but by God's perfect law. We will be judged not by the righteousness of man, but by the righteousness of God.

Author Max Lucado writes:

> All of us occasionally do what is right. A few predominately do what is right. But do any of us always do what is right? According to Paul we don't. "There is none righteous, no, not one" (Rom. 3:10 NKJV).
>
> Some may beg to differ. "I'm not perfect, Max, but I'm better than most folks. I've led a good life. I don't break the rules. I don't break hearts. I help people. I like people. Compared to others, I think I could say I'm a righteous person."
>
> I used to try that on my mother. She'd tell me that my room wasn't clean, and I'd ask her to go with me to my brother's room. His was always messier than mine. "See, my room is clean; just look at his."
>
> Never worked. She'd walk me down the hall to her room. When it came to tidy rooms, my mom was righteous. Her closet was just right.

Her bed was just right. Her bathroom was just right. Compared to hers, my room was, well, just wrong. She would show me her room and say, "This is what I mean by clean."

God does the same. He points to himself and says, "This is what I mean by righteousness."[2]

In Matthew 5:6, Jesus tells us, *"Blessed are those who hunger and thirst for righteousness, for they will be filled."* In other words, whatever you and I pursue is what we will be filled with. If we choose to pursue righteousness, we will be filled with righteousness and the promises of God. *The Message* Bible reads like this: *"You're blessed when you've worked up a good appetite for God. He's food and drink in the best meal you'll ever eat."*

When my wife, Jennifer, was facing some serious health issues, she read quite a few books on diet and eating right! Then she took it one step further and began to buy food that didn't seem very tasty—at least to me! I remember at that time that I had such a craving for "real" food. I would have to sneak out and buy it and eat it right away because Jennifer wouldn't let me keep it in the house. I learned at that time that when you really work up an appetite for something, it's amazing what you will do to fill that appetite!

> BUT RIGHTEOUSNESS IS NOT ABOUT *DOING* RIGHT; IT'S ABOUT *BEING* RIGHT WITH GOD.

In the spiritual sense, our food, our manna from heaven, the Word of God, is what we should all be craving. The righteousness of God—it's what all of humanity is longing for. God has called us to hunger and thirst after His righteousness. Have you ever been really hungry for a good meal? When you hunger for righteousness with the same passion as you hunger after food, God will fill you up!

What Does Righteousness Change?

Many people think that righteousness is about *doing* the right thing. But righteousness is not about *doing* right; it's about *being* right with God. You could get up and go to church on Sunday morning, and you'd be doing the right thing, but if you didn't really want to be there—if you were grumbling and looking at your watch the entire time—you wouldn't really *be* right, even though your actions were right. There needs to be not only a change in your actions, but a change in your attitude and in your heart's desire as well.

Imagine that you received in the mail a recall notice. It might have looked exactly like a recall notice regarding your automobile. This one was different, however, much more personal. Stamped in big red letters were the words *IMPORTANT RECALL,* under which was written the following:

The maker of all human beings is recalling all units manufactured, regardless of make or year, due to the serious defect in the primary and central component, the heart. This is due to a malfunction in the original prototype units, resulting in the reproduction of the same defect in all subsequent units. This defect has been technically termed *Subsequential internal non-morality*, or more commonly known as *SIN*, and its primary symptom is a lapse of moral judgment. If one is susceptible to loss of direction, foul vocal emissions, lack of peace and joy, or selfish behavior, then one is inflicted with the defect. The manufacturer, who is neither liable nor at fault for this defect, is providing factory-authorized repair and service, free of charge, to correct this SIN defect, at numerous locations throughout the world.[3]

The good news is that once you've been born again, all your sins are forgiven, and the Holy Spirit begins to work on your heart and change your desires. He allows you to *want* to do what is right, which makes it that much easier to actually do it.

God's Word says you are the righteousness of God in Christ (see 2 Corinthians 5:21). Get that understanding deep in your spirit. You don't just act righteously; you actually *become* the righteousness of God because of what Jesus did for you on the cross. Christ in you brings the righteousness of heaven into your heart. Now, rather than sitting around thinking, *Okay, I've got to be a better person; I've got to read my Bible more; I need to pray more; I need to volunteer more at my local church,* you no longer have only a cerebral understanding of doing right—it's in your heart, and your righteousness can come forth out of your spirit and not out of your flesh.

Once righteousness begins to seep down into your spirit, you recognize that you have been bought with a price. Your life is no longer your own, but it belongs to Him. Now the life that you live, you live by faith in Christ. It is no longer you who lives, but Christ who lives in you. A change comes in the way that you think.

David said in Psalm 51:10, *Create in me a new, clean heart, O God, filled with clean thoughts and right desires* (TLB). David had a hunger for righteousness, and he longed for God to create that righteousness in him. You see, the extraordinary life cannot be lived without the operation of righteousness in our lives. You can have all the money that you want. You can have all the status that you want. You can possess all of the material possessions that you could ever imagine, but unless you have the righteousness of God operating in you, you will be miserable. God wants to work His righteousness so deep into our hearts and lives that we know that we know that we are in right standing with Him and that every day that we get up, we understand that our lives belong to Him.

How Does Righteousness Work?

The Bible says, *"Out of the abundance of the heart the mouth speaks"* (Matthew 12:34 NKJV). Righteousness will work *through you* so that whatever is on the inside of you will begin to come out of you. God says, "Forgive." God says, "Love." God says, "Bless those who persecute you!" So many times we say, "I don't want to forgive! I don't want to love! I don't want to bless those who persecute me!" But God is working righteousness deep in your heart. He is saying, "I'll teach you forgiveness and love. I'll teach you righteousness!"

It was a small adjustment that could make a big difference. Sure, it was against NASCAR rules, but almost everyone else was doing it. So crew chief Tim Shutt crawled under the Number 20 car of Mike McLaughlin, who races on the NASCAR circuit.

WHEN JESUS CHRIST RESIDES IN YOUR HEART, HE WILL BEGIN TO BIRTH RIGHTEOUSNESS IN YOU.

"Joe [Gibbs, the team owner] is adamant that we don't cheat," says Tim, a relatively new believer who encountered Christ at a Christian retreat for participating in the racing industry. "Most teams figure that as long as you get away with it, it's not cheating.

"I said to Mike that morning in practice, 'If we're no good in practice, I'll put this piece—the illegal piece—on. Probably thirty other teams are doing it.' I was justifying it.

"I got up under the car, I got halfway through putting it on, and that verse, 'Seek ye first the kingdom of God,' came flashing in red in front of me, and whoa, that was it. I said, 'I'm leaving this up to You, God.'" Tim Shutt didn't put the piece on the car.

Mike McLaughlin won the race. It was Talladega, one of the biggest races of 2001. "When we won, the first thing that came to my mind was that verse," Tim says. "God wanted to show Himself to me."[4]

We all want to be blessed by the Lord. But the hard truth is that we won't be blessed until we learn and begin to practice righteousness in our lives. Righteousness working through us empowers us and enables us to forgive because we've been forgiven, to love because we've been loved, to bless those who persecute us, and to take on the nature and the attributes of Christ.

In Colossians 1:27, the Bible says, *For it has pleased God to tell his people that the riches and glory of Christ are for you Gentiles, too. For this is the secret: Christ lives in you, and this is your assurance that you will share in his glory* (NLT). When Jesus Christ resides in your heart, He will begin to birth righteousness in you. If there is righteousness in your heart, there will be beauty in your character. If there is beauty in your character, there will be harmony in the home. If there is harmony in the home, there will be order in the nation. And if there is order in the nation, there will be peace in the world. It seems that everyone today is seeking after peace, but true peace can only be born out of the righteousness of the Son of God—the Prince of Peace.

The peace that the world is seeking can only be found through the righteousness of Christ lived out through His people.

And so it works in our lives. Good men avoid sin because of the love of virtue. Wicked men avoid sin because of the fear of punishment. But when righteousness gets on the inside of you, you avoid sin because of a deep, burning passion to please God. When you get up every day, righteousness draws you to the Word of God. Righteousness draws you to spend time with your Creator. Righteousness woos you closer to the Lover of your soul. So don't just pursue *doing right.* Pursue knowing more intimately the Son of Righteousness, because the closer you draw to Him, the farther you will get from sin and wickedness in your life.

What Does Righteousness Do for Me?

Righteousness does many things for the believer. First, it brings about an incredible reward. Proverbs 13:21 says, *Misfortune pursues the sinner, but prosperity is the reward of the righteous.* Proverbs 15:6 declares, *The house of the righteous contains great treasure, but the income of the wicked brings them trouble.* A righteous life, lived in relationship with God, brings great prosperity. Psalm 37:25 promises, *I have never seen the righteous forsaken or their children begging bread.* Only the righteous can enjoy the fruit of their labor because of their relationship with God. The goal must continually be righteousness, which brings about the rewards of God: *The path of the righteous is like the first gleam of dawn, shining ever brighter till the full light of day* (Proverbs 4:18). The illumination of heaven, the amazing revelation of God flows to those who seek His righteousness.

Second, righteousness brings a pardon from sin and a purity of heart. Several years ago, Bob Sheffield of the Navigators told a moving story of what it means to receive God's forgiveness. Before he became a Christian, Bob played professional hockey in Canada. He was tough, loved to fight, and found himself in jail one night after a barroom brawl. Later, Bob and his wife became Christians. They accepted a temporary assignment with the Navigators in the United States.

Bob had to apply for landed immigrant status, which would allow him and his wife to continue in ministry in the United States. But because he had a criminal record, his request was denied. They decided to apply in Canada for what is called the "Queen's Pardon." Following a thorough investigation, the pardon was granted. Bob Sheffield received the following notice in the mail:

> Whereas we have since been implored on behalf of the said Robert Jones Sheffield to extend a pardon to him in respect to the convictions against him, and whereas the solicitor general here submitted a report to us, now know ye therefore, having taken these things into

consideration, that we are willing to extend the royal clemency on him, the said Robert J. Sheffield. We have pardoned, remitted, and released him of every penalty to which he was liable in pursuance thereof.[5]

On any document from that time forward on which Bob was asked if he had a criminal record, he could honestly answer no. The pardon meant that he was released from any possible punishment for the crimes, and the record of the crimes themselves was completely erased. That is the kind of pardon we have in Jesus Christ. We are set free from any penalty or punishment. When asked, the answer is, "no record, pardoned by the blood of Christ."

In Psalm 51:10, David prayed, *Create in me a pure* [clean] *heart....* Purity is born out of a relationship with God, a relationship that brings forth righteousness. Martin Luther once said, "My conscience has been taken captive by the Word of God." When righteousness begins to sink deep into your spirit, and your mind is saturated by God's Word, you will be "held captive" to a life filled with the blessing of purity.

Third, righteousness proves your individuality. A righteous person doesn't follow the crowd. A righteous man or woman of God does not live in fear of what other people will think. When God's righteousness has been birthed deep inside of you, your only concern is pleasing your Father. Many lives have been touched and changed because of the character and nature of God—and the same will be true in your life. The righteousness of God that sets you apart will begin to change the lives of those around you.

One person put it this way: "When I was a child, I was, like most children, afraid of things that go bump in the night. But I told myself, for no good reason, that monsters that lie under beds cannot break through blankets and sheets. By the time I was a teenager, I wasn't afraid any longer of what lived under my bed, but I was afraid of what my friends might have to say about the way I combed my hair. What do I fear now? I'm afraid, to put it simply, of living a life that doesn't matter. I'm afraid of leaving the world exactly as I found it, no different for my having been here." What a righteous statement! What a righteous kind of prayer: *God, don't let my life count for nothing. Lord, let it be said of me when I leave this place that I made some kind of difference.*

> LIVE YOUR LIFE SO THAT OTHERS CAN CLEARLY SEE CHRIST IN YOU.

Jesus came to seek and to save the lost. That's what righteousness still does. He came to set the captives free—and that is what righteousness can do in your life. Do you want to live an extraordinary life? Then help make someone else's life extraordinary. Do you want to live a life that is filled with joy? Then bring joy to those around you. Live as God has called you to live, a life holy and pleasing unto Him. Live your life in such a way that the world will miss you when you're gone. Live so that your coworkers will miss you. Live so that your neighbors will miss you. Live so that even those who see you at the gas station or the grocery store will miss you. Live your life so that others can clearly see Christ in you. It's not about doing good; it's about giving your life over to an awesome God so that His righteousness can work through you and lead you to the extraordinary life He has waiting for you.

Extraordinary Word

Read and/or memorize the following Scripture passages, allowing them to transform your life.

▶   [Jesus said,] *"Blessed are those who hunger and thirst for righteousness, for they will be filled"* (Matthew 5:6).

▶   *Create in me a new, clean heart, O God, filled with clean thoughts and right desires* (Psalm 51:10 TLB).

▶   *Misfortune pursues the sinner, but prosperity is the reward of the righteous* (Proverbs 13:21).

▶   *The house of the righteous contains great treasure, but the income of the wicked brings them trouble* (Proverbs 15:6).

▸ *The path of the righteous is like the first gleam of dawn, shining ever brighter till the full light of day* (Proverbs 4:18).

Extraordinary Focus

▸ What does it mean to you to have "the righteousness of God"?

▸ What has made our righteousness possible?

▸ What kinds of changes has living a life of righteousness made for you? How have you lived a life characterized by "extraordinary decency"?

Extraordinary Action

In what ways could righteousness bring about a change in the following areas of your life?

▸ Your thoughts
▸ Your speech
▸ Your actions

*The goodness of God
is the drive behind all
the blessings He daily
bestows upon us.*

A. W. Tozer

STEP 7

REWARDS:

EXTRAORDINARY INCENTIVES

MANY CORPORATIONS TODAY HAVE "INCENTIVE programs," designed to bring out the best in their employees. These programs don't exist to manipulate people, but to motivate them to do their jobs to the best of their ability. The Bible is full of incentives, designed by God to reward us when we obey His Word. These incentives go all the way back to the book of Deuteronomy, where God said, "If you'll obey Me, you'll be blessed in the city and in the country; you'll be blessed both coming in and going out. You'll be the head and not the tail, above only and not beneath—if you'll obey Me." (See Deuteronomy 28.) Those are amazing incentives! God is saying to us, "I want to show you what the rewards of your obedience will be. If you do what I tell you to do, you can't help but be blessed!"

God is an extravagant God, and He loves to reward His children. Rev. William Secker once commented, "The Lord Jesus spreads a large table every day."[1] Jesus Himself said, *"Let not your heart be troubled; you believe in God, believe also in Me. In My Father's house are many mansions"* (John 14:1–2 NKJV). Jesus didn't say that there were many "lean-to shacks" in His Father's house; He said there were many *mansions*. Why? Because the Father loves to reward His children.

Think about it this way: When the spring begins to come after a cold, dreary winter, it's amazing to see all of the flowers begin to come up out of the ground. And guess what? They're all different! God provides us with so many beautiful flowers and all of them are in different styles and colors. It's like He is trying to say to us, "Look at Me. I'm an extravagant God. I'm an abundant God! And I have created all of this beauty—just for you."

> GOD IS EXCITED ABOUT THE POSSIBILITY OF REWARDING YOU AND ME!

God didn't just create the sun and the moon and put them into the sky for our warmth and to light our days and nights. No, He had to fling billions of stars into the universe to create the Milky Way! He has created all kinds of wonders for His children, from the mountains in Colorado to the beaches in Florida and California. Different kinds of trees and different kinds of animals.

How could we ever believe that God is anything but an extravagant God?

If we do not believe that God is an extravagant God, our prayers may fall far short of His will for us. C. S. Lewis once said, "If we consider the unblushing promises of reward and the staggering nature of rewards promised by God in the gospels, it would seem that our Lord finds our desires not too strong, but too weak."[2] In *The Pilgrim's Progress*, John Bunyan wrote, "The rewards are such as should make us leap to think on them. And that we should remember with exceeding joy and never think that it is contrary to the Christian faith to rejoice and be glad for them."[3] In other words, God is excited about the possibility of rewarding you and me!

A. T. Pierson (1837–1911), powerful preacher, educator, and missionary statesman, once tried to preach on God's blessings as described in Ephesians 1–3, a section of Scripture that continually talks about our unsearchable wealth and riches in Christ. Pierson said:

> In the words of the text, "the unsearchable riches of Christ," "unsearchable" literally means riches that can never be explored. You not only cannot count or measure them, but you can form no estimate of them; and you not only can form no estimate of them, but you never can get to the end of your investigation. There is a boundless continent, a world, a universe of riches, that still lies before you, when you have

carried your search to the limits of possibility. I feel as though I had a theme, about which no man ought to speak. An archangel's tongue could do no justice to it.[4]

Pierson nevertheless tried to point out the truths about the believer's wealth as described in these three chapters. Then he told his congregation:

I sink back exhausted, in the vain attempt to set before this congregation the greatest mystery of grace that I ever grappled with. I cannot remember, in my thirty years of Gospel preaching, ever to have been confronted with a theme that more baffled every outreach of thought and every possibility of utterance than the theme that I have now attempted in the name of God to present.[5]

The Availability of Rewards

There are two types of rewards that God wants to give to His children: temporal and eternal. There are some rewards that will come to us here on earth, but there are other rewards that we can receive only when we get to heaven. God wants us to receive both kinds of rewards!

Most Christians would have no trouble believing that there are rewards waiting for them in heaven. The problem many Christians have, however, is in expecting to receive rewards here on earth.

Evangelist John R. Rice once wrote, "I once imagined I was in Heaven. Walking along with the Angel Gabriel I said, 'Gabe, what is that big building there?'

"'You'll be disappointed,' he answered. 'I don't think you want to see it.' But I insisted, and he showed me floor after floor of beautiful gifts, all wrapped and ready to be sent.

"'Gabriel, what are all these?'

"He said, I thought rather sadly, 'We wrapped these things, but people never called for them.'"[6]

Many times people have trouble believing that they deserve the rewards that God so freely offers to them. Instead of seeing themselves through the eyes of God or through the shed blood of Jesus Christ, they begin to look at all of their flaws, at their humanity, and say, "I don't deserve this."

Don't let that happen to you! Don't allow the devil to cheat you out of the rewards God wants to pour out on your life! You must overcome the "I-don't-deserve-this" mentality, because of course you don't *deserve* it! That was the whole point of Jesus' death on the cross. He died to make it possible for each of us to receive God's blessings, God's favor—but we must accept this free gift and incorporate it into our lives.

In Mark 10:29-30, Jesus said, *"I tell you the truth, … no one who has left home or brothers or sisters or mother or father or children or fields for me and the gospel will fail to receive a hundred times as much in this present age (homes, brothers, sisters, mothers, children and fields—and with them persecutions) and in the age to come, eternal life."* God wants to reward us on this side of heaven. Jesus died so that we could receive all the blessings God has for us. The nature and character of God is extravagant, beautiful, giving, *"For God so loved the world that he gave…"* (John 3:16).

There is a difference between the free gift of salvation and the rewards that God offers His children. Salvation is the free gift of God through Jesus Christ. Jesus died on the cross so that we might receive forgiveness of our sins and be able to enter a relationship with our heavenly Father. However, once we accept Jesus as our Savior and begin to walk in the ways of God, we will begin to be rewarded for following godly principles and practices. We receive the "incentives" God has put into place for following His Word and being obedient to His ways.

> WE RECEIVE THE "INCENTIVES" GOD HAS PUT INTO PLACE FOR FOLLOWING HIS WORD AND BEING OBEDIENT TO HIS WAYS.

Now, you may say, "Well, I'm not really interested in rewards." You ought to be! God is a rewarder, and everything you do for Him is going to come with a reward, whether you want it or not. The Bible says, *Work with enthusiasm, as though you were working for the Lord rather than for people. Remember that the Lord will reward each one of us for the good we do, whether we are slaves or free* (Ephesians 6:7–8 NLT). Your position in this world—whether you're male or female, black or white, Jew or Gentile, young or old—does not determine your rewards. Instead, God has developed your reward system based on the things you do that really count—the things you do unselfishly out of love for Him and in service to His kingdom.

The Acceptability of Rewards

Some Christians may wonder, *Is it really acceptable for me to receive rewards from God?* You know what? When I die, I am leaving my inheritance to my children. Why would I do that? Because they're my children, and I love them. I want them to be blessed. Proverbs 13:22 says, *A good man leaves an inheritance for his children's children.* The Bible says that if we, as mere human beings, know how to give good gifts to our children, how much more will God reward His children, whom He loves? (See Matthew 7:11.)

> [Jesus said,] *"Don't bargain with God. Be direct. Ask for what you need. This isn't a cat-and-mouse, hide-and-seek game we're in. If your child asks for bread, do you trick him with sawdust? If he asks for fish, do you scare him with a live snake on his plate? As bad as you are, you wouldn't think of such a thing. You're at least decent to your own children. So don't you think the God who conceived you in love will be even better?"*
> MATTHEW 7:9-11 MSG

The prayer of Jabez has become more well-known in recent years, and it contains an important principle: Jabez was not afraid to ask God for His blessings on his life.

> *Jabez was more honorable than his brothers. His mother had named him Jabez, saying, "I gave birth to him in pain." Jabez cried out to the God of Israel, "Oh, that you would bless me and enlarge my territory! Let your hand be with me, and keep me from harm so that I will be free from pain." And God granted his request.*
>
> 1 CHRONICLES 4:9–10

What gives you the right to ask God, like Jabez did, for His blessings on your life? The cross gives you that right. The Bible says that you are an heir of God and a joint-heir with Jesus Christ (see Romans 8:17). Jesus said, "I'll leave you with My name, and whatsoever things you ask in My name, I'll do it" (see John 14:13). You have been bought with a price, and you now have the right to approach God through His Son, Jesus Christ. The blessings and rewards of God are available to you today.

Perhaps you have never seen the rewards of God in your life. You may have rejected the idea of rewards, and yet you wonder why your needs are never met. Now is the time for change! Now is the time for you to rise up in faith, like Jabez, and cry out to the Lord, "Bless me! Enlarge my territory! Keep me from harm, and take away my pain. I want to see Your rewards come to pass in my life!"

Hebrews 11:6 tells us, *But without faith it is impossible to please Him, for he who comes to God must believe that He is, and that He is a rewarder of those who diligently seek Him* (NKJV). God's character and nature cannot change. He is a rewarder, and He will always be a rewarder. When we come to God, we must come to Him in faith, believing that He will reward us when we diligently seek His face. We must make it our goal to please Him in everything that we do. Second Corinthians 5:9 instructs us, *So we make it our goal to please Him, whether we are at home in the body or away from it. For we must all appear before the judgment seat of Christ, that each one may receive what is due him for the things done while in the body, whether good or bad.* The challenge is that we need to learn about the character, the nature, that God desires to bless. Never be ashamed of the rewards of God!

The Responsibility of Rewards

When God begins to reward His children with blessings, He expects them to be responsible stewards of the things that He has given. We are responsible to take care of the people that God places in our lives. Proverbs 19:17 promises, *He who is kind to the poor lends to the LORD, and he will reward him for what he has done.* In other words, when you are a good steward of the rewards you receive, God will bless you even further for what you have done.

Robert distinctly remembered the first time he ever went out to eat after he had accepted Christ. He found himself wanting somehow to share Jesus with the waitress who was serving his family. Then an idea came to him. If he didn't order a meal for himself, he could take that money and leave it as an extra-generous tip along with an evangelistic tract. Maybe the tip would encourage her to read the tract and come to know the Lord. So that's what they did. Before they left, they said a few words to her about how much God cared about her.

About a month later, Robert and his family were back in that same restaurant for their monthly "splurge." Through the month, Robert had prayed that God would bless them with enough extra money to be able to leave an even bigger tip along with another tract.

OBEDIENCE TO THE LORD WILL ALWAYS BRING A BLESSING IN YOUR LIFE.

Just as he had asked, God had allowed them to accumulate an extra fifty dollars that they could leave along with a booklet about salvation. That night they requested the same waitress and left her a fifty-dollar tip on a ten-dollar meal.

They returned to the restaurant one month later, very eager to see if that waitress was still working there. She was, indeed.

When she saw them, she said, "I read that little booklet you left the last time you were here." They tried not to show how excited they were to hear that. She continued, "And I prayed that prayer to receive Christ at the end of it." Of course, Robert and his family were thrilled to hear that. But she wasn't finished. "Then I called my husband on the phone and read the whole booklet to him, and he prayed that prayer, too."

At that point, Robert said, "That's wonderful! But what do you mean, you called your husband? Does he travel for a living?"

Looking embarrassed, she said, "No, my husband is in prison. He will get out in two or three years. We both want to thank you for leaving me that booklet and for being so generous. Money has been pretty scarce since he went to prison."

Over the next few years, Robert and his wife discipled this sweet waitress and saw great spiritual growth in her life. They also began to mentor her husband in prison. When he was released, he joined the church with his wife, and they were baptized together. Because Robert had acknowledged the responsibility of the rewards God had given him, he had the privilege of knowing that the lives and eternal destinies of this couple had been changed forever.

Obedience to the Lord will always bring a blessing in your life. That is why God issued such a challenge with regard to the tithe: "Bring the whole tithe into the storehouse," He told the people, "and I'll open the floodgates of heaven. See if I won't pour out such a blessing that you won't have room enough to contain it all!" (See Malachi

3:10.) God wants us to understand that He is an extraordinary, extravagant God, and when we take what He gives us and obey Him with it, He will reward us even more.

One aspect of the responsibility of rewards that many of us don't like to think about is that of *persecution*. When the disciples asked Jesus about the rewards they would receive as a result of their following Him, He was direct about the blessings they would receive:

> *Peter said to him, "We have left everything to follow you!"*
>
> *"I tell you the truth," Jesus replied, "no one who has left home or brothers or sisters or mother or father or children or fields for me and the gospel will fail to receive a hundred times as much in this present age (homes, brothers, sisters, mothers, children and fields—and with them, persecutions) and in the age to come, eternal life."*
>
> Mark 10:28-30

Many people love to quote this verse in reference to the one-hundredfold return they expect to receive, but they often forget to include those four little words, *"and with them, persecutions."* Life may not always be easy this side of heaven—we are not promised a lack of problems and difficulties once we accept Jesus Christ. But we *are* promised an extraordinary life—one that is filled with the power and presence of the Lord and all the rewards He promises as a result.

In Luke there is another challenging passage for many Christians, but it doesn't need to be:

[Jesus said,] *"Blessed are you when men hate you, when they exclude you and insult you and reject your name as evil, because of the Son of Man. Rejoice in that day and leap for joy, because great is your reward in heaven."*

LUKE 6:22-23

The persecutions that come to us in this life provide us with a great opportunity and responsibility—to respond with God's grace, love, and power and to receive the amazing rewards He has for us as a result.

The Accountability of Rewards

Whenever God begins to reward you, you need to have a system of accountability in place to maintain your integrity. Every month, without fail, I ask my wife if we have written our tithe check to the church. I've been married to her for twenty-four years, and I still ask, because there is nothing like accountability to cause God to further His blessings on our lives.

People who hold us accountable make sure that we are doing the things we need to be doing in order to receive the reward. I encourage you to have an "accountability partner" and check in with that person often to keep yourself on track. Sometimes we simply have to be obedient and trust God in faith that the rewards are on the way.

Moses experienced this. *He chose to be mistreated along with the people of God rather than to enjoy the pleasures of sin for a short time. He regarded disgrace for the sake of Christ as of greater value than the treasures of Egypt, because he was looking ahead to his reward* (Hebrews 11:25–26). Moses knew that if he stayed accountable, if he stayed on track doing the things that God had called him to do, then he would receive his reward.

Russell and Darlene Deibler were welcomed as missionaries to New Guinea in 1938 by an old and distinguished British missionary, Dr. Robert Alexander Jaffray. When, during World War II, the Japanese invaded the island, Dr. Jaffray was with them. The Japanese seized Russell and the other male missionaries, hauling them to the concentration camps. Darlene never saw her husband again. But Dr. Jaffray, being aged and ill, was allowed to remain with the women, which included Margaret Jaffray, his daughter.

Margaret was extremely careful about the foods she prepared for her father because of Dr. Jaffray's diabetic condition. She and Darlene had stockpiled as much saccharin as they could for use in recipes calling for sugar. But the supplies were very limited, for the war had cut them off from all external provisions.

One afternoon after a tiring walk, Dr. Jaffray, Margaret, and Darlene collapsed into chairs for tea. Margaret prepared tea and set the tray on a small table near her father. He helped himself to milk, and, instead of taking the saccharin, he picked up the sugar bowl and spooned one, two, and then three teaspoons of sugar into his tea. The women couldn't believe their eyes, and Margaret was horrified. "Daddy," she pleaded, "please don't do that. You know you aren't supposed to have sugar."

Remembering that he had recently been in a diabetic coma and understanding her fears, he tried to reassure her. "Muggie," he said, "I'm healed. I need this sugar for strength." He continued to use sugar, and when she begged that he not use so much, he patted her hand, saying, "It's all right, Muggie. I'm healed."

Not too many days later, the women were able to smuggle a urine specimen to a local Dutch doctor with a message: "For several days now Dr. Jaffray has been using sugar. He believes the Lord has healed him, but we would like confirmation."

A few days later a letter was smuggled back. The doctor had examined the specimen and found not a trace of sugar. Dr. Jaffray had indeed been healed.

Darlene later wrote, "We had a time of praising and thanking the Lord. He was preparing Dr. Jaffray for a time when there would be no saccharin, only scant rations of sugar. The Lord is very good to those who put their trust in Him."[7]

We serve an extraordinary, extravagant God! Continue to pursue Him and His ways, not His rewards, and in the process, you will be blessed beyond your wildest imagination.

Extraordinary Word

Read and/or memorize the following Scripture passages, allowing them to transform your life.

▸ [Jesus said,] *"Let not your heart be troubled; you believe in God, believe also in Me. In My Father's house are many mansions"* (John 14:1–2 NKJV).

▸ [Jesus said,] *"I tell you the truth … no one who has left home or brothers or sisters or mother or father or children or fields for me and the gospel will fail to receive a hundred times as much in this present age (homes, brothers, sisters, mothers, children and fields—and with them, persecutions) and in the age to come, eternal life"* (Mark 10:29-30).

▸ *Work with enthusiasm, as though you were working for the Lord rather than for people. Remember that the Lord will reward each one of us for the good we do, whether we are slaves or free* (Ephesians 6:7–8 NLT).

Extraordinary Focus

▶ Have you ever had trouble believing in the "acceptability" of God's rewards in your life? Why or why not?

▶ The Bible says that God will reward us when we come to Him in faith and seek His face. In what ways do you seek God's face in faith?

▶ What does the idea of the "responsibility" and "accountability" of rewards mean to you? How are you responsible and accountable for the blessings that God has given you?

Extraordinary Action

What rewards has God given *you?* In a notebook or personal journal, list as many as you can think of and then write a prayer to the Lord, thanking Him for His extraordinary incentives. What can you do with those rewards that would be a blessing to other people?

If you read history,
you will find that the
Christians who did
most for the present
world were precisely
those who thought
most of the next.

C. S. Lewis

STEP 8
RAPTURE:

EXTRAORDINARY REUNION

J ONATHAN HAD BEEN PROMISED A NEW PUPPY FOR his tenth birthday, but he had a tough time choosing between a dozen likely candidates at the neighborhood pet shop. Finally he decided upon one nondescript, shaggy pup who was wagging his tail furiously.

Why that one? Jonathan explained, "I want the one with the happy ending!"

God wants you to live an extraordinary life here on earth, and afterward to go on to an extraordinary life in heaven—the greatest "happy ending" you could ever know.

My family and I have lived in the same house for many years. I'll sometimes refer to it as "our house," but more often I refer to it as "home." What makes it home isn't the address or the lot or the garage or the architecture. What makes it home is the people.

You may live in a bigger or newer or better house than we live in, but as nice as your house may be, I would never refer to your house as "home" because the people who are most important to me don't live there. So what makes home home is the people and the relationships.

WHAT MAKES HEAVEN HEAVEN IS GOD.

And what makes heaven heaven is not streets made out of gold, great fountains, lots of fun, and no smog. That all may well be. But actually, I think that heaven is far greater than our wildest imagination. The same God who designed the best of everything in this world, also designed heaven, only He took it to a far greater extent than anything we've ever seen. *But as it is written: "Eye has not seen / nor ear heard, nor have entered into the heart of man / the things which God has prepared for those who love Him"* (1 Corinthians 2:9 NKJV). Yet, that's still not what makes heaven heaven.

What makes heaven heaven is God. It is being there with Him. With His presence come peace and contentment, a fulfillment, a sense that all is well. That is also a contentment that bubbles over into the rest of life. We can anticipate this future in the presence of God, we can be with Him in a place where everything He wants happens the way He wants it to happen. And that affects this life, as well.

All Christians who die go immediately to be in the presence of the Lord, but there is coming a day when Jesus will return to this earth, and an extraordinary reunion will take place between the saints who are still living on this planet and those who have gone on to heaven. What an amazing day that will be!

In the original Greek language, the word *rapture* does not appear in the New Testament. Many theologians have debated whether or not a second coming of Jesus will actually take place. But the apostle Paul references being "caught away" to be with the Lord. Jesus refers to His Second Coming. The Bible is not silent about the topic of the Rapture.

In the days of Paul, the church at Thessalonica was very concerned about what had happened to those Christians who had already died and when Jesus would return. The apostle Paul wrote to comfort them with the fact that the Rapture would one day take place.

> *Brothers, we do not want you to be ignorant about those who fall asleep* [or die]. *... We believe that Jesus died and rose again and so we believe that God will bring with Jesus those who have fallen asleep in him. According to the Lord's own word, we tell you that we who are still alive, who are left till the coming of the Lord, will certainly not precede those who have fallen asleep. For the Lord himself will come down from heaven, with a loud command, with the voice of the archangel and*

> *with the trumpet call of God, and the dead in*
> *Christ will rise first. After that, we who are still*
> *alive and are left will be caught up together with*
> *them in the clouds to meet the Lord in the air.*
> *And so we will be with the Lord forever. Therefore*
> *encourage each other with these words.*
>
> 1 THESSALONIANS 4:13–18

We are not to be afraid of the Second Coming of the Lord; we are to look forward to it with anticipation! Jesus said that He will come quickly; He is coming to take us away from the trials of this earth. In Revelation 3:10, He says, *"Because you have kept My command to persevere, I also will keep you from the hour of trial which shall come upon the whole world, to test those who dwell on the earth"* (NKJV). We will all be changed in a moment, in the twinkling of an eye. We will be instantly swept up to heaven to be reunited with all the Christians throughout the ages who trusted in Jesus Christ and have gone on to receive their final reward in Him.

John Bartlett has written these words to give Christians everywhere the assurance of Jesus' return:

> March 11, 1942, on Corregidor, a sixty-two-year-old Army officer, with his family, secretly slipped away from the Philippines and in a minor miracle made their way down to Australia. Before General MacArthur left the islands, he said, "I will return." Two-and-a-half

years later, October 20, 1944, he stood again on the soil of the Philippines and said, "This is the voice of freedom. People of the Philippines, I have returned."

Now if you think a man can have that kind of credibility, and if you can appreciate that quality in a man, I'll tell you that Jesus Christ, the God-Man, has made the same promise far more credible than any human being will ever be. If you wrestle with the truth of Jesus' return, wrestle no longer. If you accept the historic fact of His ascension, then you have no room to doubt His historic, yet future, return. It will occur.[1]

What Do You Need to Do?

What do you need to do to prepare for the Rapture? It's very simple. You need to be ready. The Bible tells us to be ready at all times because we do not know when Jesus will return for us. *"You also must be ready, because the Son of Man will come at an hour when you do not expect him"* (Matthew 24:44). In Luke 19:13, Jesus said, *"Do business ... until I get back"* (NCV). We are to be about the Father's business, always pressing in for more of His presence, more of His blessing, more of His rewards, and readying ourselves for the day when we will see Him face-to-face. As believers, we have been given the greatest story ever told, and we need to be telling that story to others. When Jesus returns, let Him "catch you" being a good witness for Him, standing strong in your faith, and sharing His Word with others.

We also need to keep learning and growing in the Lord. We've got to put ourselves in a place of discipline and worship, aligned with the local church, Jesus' Bride, for whom He will return. Hebrews 10:23–25 instructs us:

> *Now we can look forward to the salvation God has promised us. There is no longer any room for doubt, and we can tell others that salvation is ours, for there is no question that he will do what he says.*
>
> *In response to all he has done for us, let us outdo each other in being helpful and kind to each other and in doing good.*
>
> *Let us not neglect our church meetings, as some people do, but encourage and warn each other, especially now that the day of his coming back again is drawing near.*
>
> HEBREWS 10:23-25 TLB

U.S. astronaut Shannon Lucid desperately wanted to go home. She had spent six months on the Russian Mir space station, from March until September 1996. Her ride home was delayed six weeks by two hurricanes and assorted mechanical problems with the shuttle booster rockets, making her stay in space the longest of any

American astronaut, man or woman. Nevertheless, she faced each setback with patient good cheer and a stiff upper lip.

But as the days wore on, she knew where she would rather be. Eventually she admitted that she wanted to return home to see her family, to feel the sun and wind on her face—and to check out the new books published in the last few months! Prior to being picked up for her return to Earth by the space shuttle Atlantis, Shannon joked, "You can rest assured that I am not going to be on the wrong side of that hatch when they close it!"

> THE CLOSER I GET TO GOD WHILE I'M STILL ON THIS EARTH, THE MORE I ANTICIPATE BEING WITH HIM FOREVER!

Just as Shannon was not willing to let anything come between her and her trip back home, so we, too, must be sure to be ready for our trip back "home." The Word tells us: Don't forsake the things that you know to do! Look forward to the day of celebration that the coming of the Lord will bring. It's going to be a day of incredible reunion.

Reunion with God

Paul wrote to the Thessalonians, *We who are still alive and are left will be caught up together with them in the clouds to meet the Lord in the air. And so we will be with the Lord forever* (1 Thessalonians 4:17). Think about that. We will meet our glorious Lord and Savior face-to-face! What a joy it will be to meet our Creator, the One who died to save us, the One who's given us the opportunity to live and move and have our being. I can't think of anything greater, can you? The closer I get to God while I'm still on this earth, the more I anticipate being with Him forever!

Writer Joni Eareckson Tada once recalled the comment of a young boy at the end of a retreat for the handicapped when participants were asked to tell what the week had meant to them:

> Little freckle-faced, red-haired Jeff raised his hand. We were so excited to see what Jeff would say, because Jeff had won the hearts of us all at the family retreat. Jeff was Down's syndrome. He took the microphone, put it right up to his mouth, and said, "Let's go home!"
>
> Later, his mother told me, "Jeff really missed his dad back home. His dad couldn't come to the family retreat because he had to work." Even though Jeff had had a great time, a fun-filled week, he was ready to go home because he missed his daddy.
>
> This world is pleasant enough. But would we really want it to go on forever as a family retreat? I don't think so. I'm with Jeff. I miss my Daddy, my Abba Father. My heart is longing to go home.[2]

The hope of being with God, of seeing Him face-to-face and enjoying His presence forever, is one of the greatest joys of the Christian faith!

Reunion with Our Loved Ones

Not only will we meet our Lord face-to-face on that amazing day, but we will also meet all of our loved ones who have accepted Jesus Christ and gone on to be with Him.

In his book on heaven, evangelist Dwight L. Moody writes, "When I was a boy, I thought of heaven as a great, shining city, with vast walls and domes and spires, and with nobody in it except white-robed angels, who were strangers to me. By and by my little brother died, and I thought of a great city with walls and domes and spires, and one little fellow that I was acquainted with. He was the only one I knew at that time. Then another brother died, and there were two that I knew. Then my acquaintances began to die, and the flock continually grew. But it was not till I had sent one of my own little children to his Heavenly Parent—God—that I began to think I had a little in myself. A second went; a third went; a fourth went; and by that time I had so many acquaintances in heaven that I did not see any more walls and domes and spires. I began to think of the residents of the celestial city as my friends. And now so many of my acquaintances have gone there, that it sometimes seems to me that I know more people in heaven than I do here on earth."[3]

In June 1977, my precious grandmother went to heaven, and it had a tremendous effect on my life. At the time, I was strung out on drugs and running from God, but I would go over to her house and sit with her. I was attracted to the presence of God in her life, and I didn't even know it. When she died in 1977, I came face-to-face with eternity. Three weeks later I gave my life to Christ. Now, every time I think of the great reunion that will take place on that glorious day, I can't wait to meet her again and share with her what an impact she made on my life.

> YOU WILL SPEND ALL OF ETERNITY WITH THEM, BASKING IN GOD'S PRESENCE AND ENJOYING HIM FOREVER.

Vince Havner once painted a powerful picture of heaven with these words:

> "When I started out as a boy preaching, Father went along. Then when I got old enough to go by myself, he'd meet me at the little railroad station in Newton, North Carolina. I can see him standing there by that old Ford roadster, in that old blue serge suit that hadn't been pressed since the day he bought it.
>
> "When I'd go up to him, the first thing he'd ask me would be, 'How did you get along?'

"It's been a long time, and one of these days when my train rounds into Grand Central Station in glory, I think he'll be there—not in the old blue serge suit, but in the robes of glory. I wouldn't be surprised if the first thing he'd say would be, 'How did you get along?'

"I think I'll say, 'Pretty well, and I owe a lot to you for it.' Then I think I'd say, 'You remember back in the country when I was a little boy, no matter where I was in the afternoon I was supposed to be back by sundown. It's been a long trip, Dad, but here I am by the grace of God, home before dark.'"[4]

Which of your loved ones have gone on before you to be with the Lord? Rest assured, my friend, that you will see them again. You will spend all of eternity with them, basking in God's presence and enjoying Him forever.

A woman was diagnosed with a terminal illness and had been given three months to live. As she was getting her things in order, she contacted her pastor and asked him to come to her house to discuss some of her final wishes.

She told him which songs she wanted sung at her funeral service, what Scriptures she would like to have read, and what outfit she wanted to be buried in. She requested to be buried with her favorite Bible.

As the pastor prepared to leave, the woman suddenly remembered something else. "There's one more thing," she said excitedly.

"What's that?" asked the pastor.

"This is important," the woman said. "I want to be buried with a fork in my right hand."

The pastor stood looking at the woman, not knowing quite what to say.

The woman explained, "In all my years of attending church socials and potluck dinners, when the dishes of the main course were being cleared, someone would inevitably lean over and say, 'Keep your fork.' It was my favorite part of the meal, because I knew that something better was coming—like velvety chocolate cake or deep-dish apple pie.

"So, when people see me in that casket with a fork in my hand and they ask, 'What's with the fork?' I want you to tell them: 'Keep your fork. The best is yet to come!'"

This life is not all there is. Yes, God wants you to live an extraordinary life here on earth, but He also looks forward to your extraordinary life with Him throughout all eternity. The book of Revelation provides a glimpse into this amazing life that awaits all of us who have been redeemed by the blood of the Lamb.

The four living creatures, each having six wings, were full of eyes around and within. And they do not rest day or night, saying:

"Holy, holy, holy,
Lord God Almighty,
Who was and is and is to come!"
Whenever the living creatures give glory and
honor and thanks to Him who sits on the throne,
who lives forever and ever, the twenty-four elders
fall down before Him who sits on the throne and
worship Him who lives forever and ever, and cast
their crowns before the throne, saying:
"You are worthy, O Lord,
To receive glory and honor and power;
For You created all things,
And by Your will they exist and were created."
                                Revelation 4:8–11 nkjv

In heaven, we will begin to understand that everything we've ever experienced in this life—the very greatest moments in our lives on earth—cannot compare one iota with what we will experience in heaven! None of the things we experience in this life will hold a shred of meaning for us when we come face-to-face with our Creator and realize that we are to live for all eternity in His presence!

And I heard a loud voice from the throne saying,
"Now the dwelling of God is with men, and he
will live with them. They will be his people, and
God himself will be with them and be their God.
He will wipe every tear from their eyes. There will

be no more death or mourning or crying or pain,
for the old order of things has passed away."
REVELATION 21:3–4

As Hazel Felleman put it in her beautiful poem entitled "Heaven":

> Think of—
> Stepping on shore, and finding it Heaven!
> Of taking hold of a hand, and finding it God's hand.
> Of breathing a new air, and finding it celestial air.
> Of feeling invigorated, and finding it immortality.
> Of passing from storm to tempest to an unknown calm.
> Of waking up, and finding it Home.[5]

Extraordinary Word

Read and/or memorize the following Scripture passages, allowing them to transform your life.

▶ *"You also must be ready, because the Son of Man will come at an hour when you do not expect him"* (Luke 12:40).

- *We who are still alive and are left will be caught up together with them in the clouds to meet the Lord in the air. And so we will be with the Lord forever* (1 Thessalonians 4:17).

- *We believe that Jesus died and rose again and so we believe that God will bring with Jesus those who have fallen asleep in him* (1 Thessalonians 4:14).

- *"Now the dwelling of God is with men, and he will live with them. They will be his people, and God himself will be with them and be their God. He will wipe every tear from their eyes. There will be no more death or mourning or crying or pain, for the old order of things has passed away"* (Revelation 21:3–4).

Extraordinary Focus

- How can a view of your future life in heaven help you to live a more abundant life here on earth? Be as specific as you can.

- What loved ones have gone ahead to be with the Lord and are now looking forward to seeing you in heaven? What do you believe that amazing day of reunion will be like?

▸ What are you doing to be prepared for the day when Jesus comes to take you home?

Extraordinary Action

What specific things do you want to be "caught" doing when Jesus returns? In a notebook or in your personal journal, write out your commitment to make these actions a part of your life—starting today!

*The true call of a
Christian is not to
do extraordinary
things, but to do
ordinary things in an
extraordinary way.*

DEAN STANLEY

CONCLUSION

YOU CAN EXPERIENCE GOD'S AMAZING, ABUNDANT life here on earth, and look forward to a glorious life with Him in the future! The eight principles outlined in this book will lead you to an abundant, extraordinary life.

Receiving a *revelation* of who God is and understanding His extraordinary love for you is the first step in living an extraordinary life. True *repentance* follows—turning away from the things of this world and turning to God, completely and wholly. *Renewing* your mind is the next step, which will draw you closer to God. Choosing your *relationships* with care will become a priority, and right relationships will bring you closer to Him. You will walk out your extraordinary life with *routines*—step-by-step, day-by-day acts of following Jesus. Then you must live in *righteousness*, letting go and letting God work through you. *Rewards* will follow you as you follow Him. *Rapture* is the final step in walking with God because that is when we meet God, our Creator, face-to-face and receive a full revelation of who He is and how much He loves us.

God's extraordinary life awaits you! Aren't you ready to experience it today? Make a decision to begin your journey to experience the extraordinary life that God has waiting for you. As Jesus said, *"I have come that they may have life, and that they may have it more abundantly"* (John 10:10 NKJV).

Prayer

Lord Jesus, thank You for dying for my sins. Today, I repent of my sins. I confess that You are the Lord of my life. Thank You for forgiving me of my sins and for giving me a new life. (Romans 10:9-10; 2 Corinthians 5:17) *Amen.*

NOTES

Step 1 Revelation: Extraordinary God

1. David Redding, *Jesus Makes Me Laugh with Him* (Grand Rapids: Zondervan, 1978), 10.

2. Connie Willems, "Captivated by God," *Discipleship Journal* (Nov./Dec. 2002): 72.

3. J. I. Packer, *Knowing God* (Downers Grove, IL: InterVarsity Press, 1993), 20-21.

Step 2 Repentance: Exercising Extraordinary Faith

1. Frederica Mathewes-Green, *The Illumined Heart: The Ancient Christian Path of Transformation* (Orleans, MA: Paraclete Press, 2001), 102.

2. Robert J. Morgan, *Nelson's Complete Book of Stories, Illustrations, and Quotes* (Nashville: Thomas Nelson, 2000), 662.

3. Ibid.

4. Lesslie Newbigin (d. 1996), *Mission in Christ's Way* (Cincinnati, OH: Friendship Press, 1988), 45.

5. Cedric Pulford, "Repentant Pilferers Return Hotel Towels and Cash after Sermon on Theft," *Ecumenical News International* (June 12, 2001): 21-23.

Step 3 Renewal: Extraordinary Change

1. Corroborated by Kelly Callaghan, prayer and courier coordinator, Open Doors USA. Open Doors USA serves the persecuted church worldwide.

2. Wilbur M. Smith, *Profitable Bible Study* (Grand Rapids: Baker Book House, 1963), 61.

3. Robert J. Morgan, *From This Verse* (Nashville: Thomas Nelson, 1998), 138.

4. Rick Warren, *The Purpose Driven Life* (Grand Rapids: Zondervan, 2002), 233.

5. Charles R. Swindoll, *Growing Strong in the Seasons of Life* (Grand Rapids: Zondervan, 1994), 92.

6. Charles H. Spurgeon, *John Ploughman's Talks* (New York: Sheldon & Company, n.d.), 139.

Step 4 Relationships: Extraordinary Connections

1. Cited in William M. Anderson, *The Faith That Satisfies* (New York: Loizeaux Brothers, 1948), 165.

2. J. Hudson Taylor, *To China with Love* (Minneapolis: Dimension Books, n.d.), 89–91.

3. Gordon MacDonald, *Restoring Your Spiritual Passion* (Nashville: Thomas Nelson, 1986), 176–177.

4. George Barna, *Grow Your Church from the Outside In* (Ventura, CA: Regal Books, 2002), 11-12.

5. Morgan, 135.

6. Charles H. Spurgeon, *Lectures to My Students* (Grand Rapids: Zondervan, 1954), 337.

7. Morgan, 135.

8. Bill Bright, "How to Tell Others About Christ," *Worldwide Challenge* (April 1993): 17.

Step 5 Routines: Extraordinary Discipline

1. James Belasco, *Teaching the Elephant to Dance: The Manager's Guide to Empowering Change* (New York, NY: Plume, 1991), 91.

2. Tim Whitmire, "Rookie Police Officer on Routine Patrol Nabs Fugitive," *Courier Journal* (June 2, 2003): 15.

3. Morgan, 398.

4. Morgan, 398.

5. Alfred Armand, comp., *Distilled Wisdom* (Upper Saddle River, New Jersey: Prentice-Hall, Inc., 1964), 186.

6. John Cook, comp., *The Book of Positive Quotations* (New York: Random House, Gramercy Books, 1999), 456.

7. Auriel Douglas and Michael Strumph, comps., *Webster's Dictionary of Quotations* (New York: Random House, Gramercy Books, 1998), 5.

8. Morgan, 398.

9. Dr. Julius Segal, *Winning Life's Toughest Battles: Roots of Human Resilience* (New York, NY: Ivy Books, 1987), 82.

10. Ibid.

11. Morgan, 398.

Step 6 Righteousness: Extraordinary Decency

1. Herb Miller, *Actions Speak Louder Than Verbs* (Nashville: Abingdon Press, 1989), 15.

2. Max Lucado, *Traveling Light* (Nashville: Word, 2001), 101.

3. Rick Ezell, *Seven Sins of Highly Defective People* (Grand Rapids: Kregel, 2006), 22.

4. Victor Lee, "Sports Spectrum," *Men of Integrity* (May/June 2002): 13-14.

5. Morgan, 729.

Step 7 Rewards: Extraordinary Incentives

1. William Secker, *The Nonsuch Professor in His Meridian Splendor* (Chicago: Fleming H. Revell Co., 1899), 151.

2. C. S. Lewis, *The Weight of Glory* (San Francisco: Harper San Francisco, 1951), 88.

3. John Bunyan, *The Pilgrim's Progress* (New York: A. L. Burt Company, 1909), 20.

4. A. T. Pierson, *The Gospel: Its Heart, Heights, and Hopes*, vol. 1 (Grand Rapids: Baker Book House, 1978), 220.

5. Ibid, 234.

6. John R. Rice, "Go Ahead and Ask!" *Moody Magazine* (January 1977): 61.

7. Darlene Deibler Rose, *Evidence Not Seen: One Woman's Miraculous Faith in a Japanese P.O.W. Camp* (Carlisle, UK: OM Publishing, 1988), 48–49.

Step 8 Rapture: Extraordinary Reunion

1. John Bartlett, *Bartlett's Familiar Quotations, 17th Edition* (New York: Little, Brown and Company, 2002), 685.

2. Joni Eareckson Tada, *Heaven* (Grand Rapids: Zondervan, 2001), 22.

3. D. L. Moody, *Heaven* (Chicago: Moody Press, n.d.), 32.

4. Cited in Vince Havner, "Heaven," *Christianity Today* (November 7, 1986): 45.

5. Hazel Felleman, *The Best Loved Poems of the American People* (New York: Doubleday, 1936), 13.

ABOUT THE AUTHOR

Mark Crow and his wife, Jennifer, pastor Victory Church, in Oklahoma City, which they founded in 1994. Mark's ministry philosophy was not to build a church, but to build people to live life victoriously in Jesus. With over 8,000 members, 12,000 decisions for Christ, and churches planted in other cities across America, Mark's motto, "You were born for victory," is reflected not on a church wall, but on the hearts and in the lives of men and women.

FURTHER CONNECTION

Now that you have taken your first steps toward *Extraordinary Living*, we encourage you to continue your journey by "plugging in" to your local church body.

For more information on materials and classes from Victory Life Ministries, contact us online at:

www.vlmokc.org

Or call us directly at:

(405) 717-1256

Victory Church is located at:

4300 North MacArthur, Oklahoma City, OK 73122

For information on the weekly TV show or information about Mark Crow and Victory Church, visit the church's Web site at:

www.victorychurch.tv.

VICTORY
CHURCH.TV

The following are available wherever fine books are sold.

Secrets of the Second Mile
How to Overcome Life's Obstacles
and Live in Victory
1-933188-03-0   978-1-9331880-3-4

The race of life is often run through the difficult
terrain of hardship, challenges, and conflict. In
Secrets of the Second Mile, Mark Crow combines
his own life's experiences with biblical principles
to share how you are designed to finish the race of
life—victoriously!

Mastering Your Storms
Navigating the Trials of Life Effectively
0-9753036-5-1   978-0-9753036-5-8

In *Mastering Your Storms*, author Mark Crow
equips us with effective strategies and understanding that enable us to prepare for the storms
and trials of life with biblical insight and wisdom.